Dear Frien<

If you are reading this devotional, it
going through a tough time. Whether you are grieving the loss
of a loved one, dealing with the end of a relationship, or facing
some other significant change or challenge in your life, I want
to extend my deepest sympathies to you. Grief and tough
times can be really hard to handle, especially when you're still
figuring out who you are and what you want in life.

This devotional is meant to be a source of support and
guidance as you navigate the ups and downs of grief and
tough times. It's not going to give you all the answers or make
everything better, but it will offer you encouragement, hope,
and practical tools for coping with your emotions and moving
forward.

Inside these pages, you'll find reflections, prayers, and other
spiritual practices that can help you find meaning and healing
in your grief. You'll also read the words and stories of others
who have gone through tough times and found ways to cope
and keep going.

I hope that this devotional will be a source of comfort and
strength for you as you journey through grief and tough times.
Remember that you're not alone, and that there are people
who care about you and are here to support you. May you find
solace in the love and care of those around you, and may you
find hope and healing in the days ahead.

With heartfelt compassion,
Annalise D Mitchell

CONTENTS

PART 1:
GRIEF, LOSS AND THE LORD

Day 1: Jesus Wept Too
"Jesus wept" John 11:35 NLT.

"Jesus wept" (John 11:35) is the shortest verse in the Bible. I often wondered why it was there or what value it added to the scriptures to note such a minor detail. Does it really need its own verse? But recently, I realized how remarkable John 11:35 was. Why? Because Jesus, fully God and fully man, the one who was there at the beginning of creation, the Savior of the world - He grieved.

He didn't just shed a tear; he wept. John 11:35 shows the humanity of Jesus as He wept for the death of his friend Lazarus, and He wept for the sisters of Lazarus. Jesus experienced the heartache of loss.

Logically, we can define loss as: *"the harm or privation resulting from losing or being separated from someone or something" -Marian Webster dictionary.* A person may understand the concept of loss, but it often isn't until someone is smack dab in the middle of loss that they know the emotions one experiences in the midst of loss. The empty feeling, the sadness - the ache. It can feel as if a giant pit has been dug in your heart, an uncontrollable and gut-wrenching sense.

My friend, dealing with loss is tough, it's messy, and the emotions are unpredictable. Loss can lead you to many spaces in your heart and mind. As you walk through this valley, remember that Jesus understands. He experienced loss, rejection, abandonment, and even betrayal. He grieved, just like you do now. He is a personal God,
who knows how you feel, and weeps with you.
My friend, it's okay to weep too.

Jesus, my heart is heavy. It hurts.
This loss is tough, and I feel broken.
Lord, thank you for being with me at this moment.
Make me aware of your presence; amen.

WHAT LOSS ARE YOU GOING THROUGH RIGHT NOW? HOW DOES YOUR HEART FEEL?

HOW DO YOU THINK JESUS WOULD RESPOND TO YOUR FEELINGS?

_____

_____

_____

_____

_____

_____

_____

_____

_____

_____

_____

_____

_____

_____

Day 2: Come to Me.

"Then Jesus said, 'Come to me, all of you who are weary and carry heavy burdens, and I will give you rest.'"

(Jesus, I come to You broken, tired, and sad.
I can't walk through this loss on my own.)

"Take my yoke upon you.'"

(I submit my heart to you.)

"'Let me teach you, because I am humble and gentle at heart, and you will find rest for your souls.'"
- Matthew 11:28-29 NLT.

(Teach me to trust you and rest in Your love as you heal my soul.
Amen)

"He heals the brokenhearted and bandages their wounds."
- Psalms 147:3 NLT.

(Lord, I know you are with me during this season of loss.
You see my broken heart, you hold it, and I trust that you will heal it.
Amen)

IF YOU COULD TEXT GOD RIGHT NOW, WHAT WOULD YOU TEXT?

HOW DO YOU THINK
HE WOULD REPLY?

_____

_____

_____

_____

_____

_____

_____

_____

_____

_____

_____

_____

_____

Day 3. Blessed Are Those Who Mourn?

"Blessed are those who mourn, for they shall be comforted."
- Matthew 5:4 ESV.

Picture this, a large crowd has gathered along the mountainside, and people have come from all over to hear this man called Jesus preach. Jesus stood up and in his first public sermon, said this; *"Blessed are those who mourn, for they shall be comforted."* *(Matt 4:4 ESV).*

Wait, what? Blessed are those who mourn? Hey Jesus, I'm mourning right now.... and I don't feel very blessed. Why would Jesus say that?

Here is the thing, Jesus was not saying you are blessed because you mourn, He was stating that you are blessed because you will be comforted. You may say, "Well, I would much rather not mourn and skip the comforting." Unfortunately, we live in a broken world and bad stuff happens, even to people who love Jesus. Jesus knew that in this world we would mourn, we would have trials, and we would experience broken hearts. On that mountainside, Jesus validated the process of mourning and promised that we would be comforted.

The God who created the stars, formed the mountains, and spoke the galaxies into existence; promises to comfort you. That comfort may look like His Spirit filling you with peace as you make hard decisions. He may even use the people He has placed around you to comfort you during this difficult season. No matter what you are going through, take a moment to stop and be still before the Lord. Bring your broken heart to Him, and ask for His peace to fill your heart.

Jesus, thank you for Your promise to bring me comfort during this season.
I ask that you will fill me with Your peace. Please show me where You are in this time of loss. Amen.

GOD, I FEEL...

Day 4. Blessed

"Blessed are the poor in spirit, for theirs is the kingdom of heaven."
(Jesus, my spirit depends on you, thank you that the kingdom of heaven is a part of my inheritance.)

"Blessed are those who mourn, for they shall be comforted."
(Thank you for being my comforter in this season of mourning. Lord, open my eyes to see and feel your comfort.)

"Blessed are the meek, for they shall inherit the earth."
(Lord, I choose to walk humbly with You,
thank you that the earth is a part of my inheritance.)

"Blessed are those who hunger and thirst for righteousness,
for they shall be satisfied."
(Jesus, thank you for Your promise that if I seek you, I will be satisfied. Lord, I want to hunger and thirst for Your righteousness!)

"Blessed are the merciful, for they shall receive mercy."
(Jesus, I forgive those who have hurt me. Teach me to walk in forgiveness, as You have forgiven me.)

"Blessed are the pure in heart, for they shall see God."
(Lord, purify my heart.)

"Blessed are the peacemakers, for they shall be called sons of God."
- Matthew 5:3-9 ESV.
(Father, teach me to be a peacemaker. I give you my anxiety and replace it with Your peace.)

THANK THE LORD FOR THE THINGS YOU HAVE SEEN HIM DO IN YOUR LIFE:

Day 5. Even in The Valley

*"Even though I walk through the valley of the shadow of death,
I will fear no evil, for you are with me; your rod and your staff, they
comfort me." - Psalm 23:4 ESV.*

David, once a lowly shepherd who became king of Israel,
wrote psalm 23. Psalms 23 depicts God as a shepherd, caring for us,
his sheep. At first, this Psalm sounds so nice and peaceful, "He leads
me beside still waters" (Psalms 23:2) and "He restores my soul."
(Psalms 23:3), but the leisurely stroll comes crashing to a halt when
we get to the valley of the shadow of death.

The setting that David depicts is one of despair, fear, and death.
Not a valley one would like to vacation in, that's for sure. But in this
valley, David gives us a clear image of God as our shepherd, herding
us through the valley, protecting us, and comforting us.

As a shepherd, David knew that a good shepherd doesn't just get to
the top of the hill, look down into the valley, then turn to his sheep
and say, "Well, good luck! Hope you all make it out on the other
side." No, a good shepherd is in the valley with his sheep, fending off
prey with his staff and comforting his sheep with his voice. You may
be in a valley right now, but God has not sent you into this valley
alone.
He is with you! Life will be full of valleys,
but the Lord will always be with you.

As you walk through the valley, remember there will be
beautiful mountain tops and green pastures again.
The calm streams and pleasant trails will come again, and guess
what?
The Lord will be your shepherd in those seasons too.
He will never leave you or forsake you.

*Lord, Thank you for being a good shepherd and being with me in this
valley, and I trust you to lead me out of it. I will praise You in this valley,
and I will praise you on the mountain tops; amen.*

IF YOU COULD TEXT GOD RIGHT NOW, WHAT WOULD YOU TEXT HIM?

Day 6. My Shepherd.

"The Lord is my shepherd; I shall not want.

(Lord, You are my shepherd; I trust that You will provide for me.)

He makes me lie down in green pastures.

(I rest in Your provision and safety.)

He leads me beside still waters.

(Thank you for Your peace, I give You my anxiety and fear.)

He restores my soul.

(I trust that You will mend my broken heart.)

He leads me in paths of righteousness for his name's sake.

(I trust the plans that You have for me, I choose to follow You, and may Your name be glorified.)

Even though I walk through the valley of the shadow of death, I will fear no evil, for you are with me; your rod and your staff, they comfort me.
- Psalm 23:1-4 ESV.

(Even in this valley I choose to trust you, thank you for protecting and comforting me. I give you my fears and anxiety.)

GOD, I FEEL…

Day 7. It's Okay, Not to be Okay.

"O Lord, you have examined my heart and know everything about me!
You know when I sit down or stand up. You know my thoughts even
when I'm far away." - Psalm 139:1-2 NLT.

"How are you doing?" is possibly the most dreaded question
of many people walking through a season of loss. How does one
answer that question? Truthfully? Or do you just cover it with a
blanket statement like, "eh, I'm doing okay." Your answer could
depend on who's asking. Or does one bear the wounds of their heart
to anyone? Or do you try to distract yourself from your real feelings?
Regardless of how you may answer the question to a friend or an
acquaintance, let me ask you this; How would you respond if God
asked, "How are you doing?" Would you be honest with Him?
Or would you reply how you think He would want you to reply?

Can I tell you something? He already knows your deep-down
thoughts and feelings, and guess what? He is okay with you,
not being okay. Looking at the scriptures, you will see a common
theme running throughout the entire Bible; God will never leave or
forsake you. He already knows your thoughts, and the Holy Spirit
longs to comfort you in your weakness. Be honest with God; he's not
expecting you to come to him as a perfect person. If you are angry,
tell him; if you are sad, let him know. Guess what? He already knows
and is waiting for you to come to him. He hears your cries and longs
to comfort you in this season. It's okay not to be okay.

Lord, I am thankful I can be real with you,
even though I may not completely understand how I feel.
Lord, teach me to draw near to you and trust you with my heart.
Thank you for Your promise to heal my broken heart, amen.

SO, HOW ARE YOU DOING? WRITE AN HONEST LETTER TO GOD.

Day 8. You Know Me

"O Lord, you have examined my heart and know everything about me!"

(Lord, you know exactly what is going on in my heart; I don't even need to explain how I feel.)

"You know when I sit down or stand up."

(Thank you for the way You care about me and what I am doing.)

"You know my thoughts even when I'm far away."

(Help me understand my thoughts, I am so glad You know what I am thinking and how I am feeling.)

"You see me when I travel and when I rest at home."

(You see me! Forgive me for ever believing that You do not care.)

"You know everything I do."

(You really know me!)

" You know what I am going to say even before I say it, Lord." - Psalms 139:1-6 NLT

(Lord, you know me! Help my words to honor you and those around me.)

WHAT ARE YOUR THOUGHTS TODAY?

_____

_____

_____

_____

_____

_____

_____

_____

_____

_____

_____

_____

_____

_____

Day 9. Why?

"For my thoughts are not your thoughts, neither your ways my ways, declares the Lord." - Isaiah 55:8 ESV.

Why? Why did God let this happen? Why didn't He stop it? Why did this have to happen to me? Why didn't God do a miracle and stop this from happening? Honestly, I don't know why... I've seen God work miracles, I've seen people healed from sickness, and I've seen broken families restored. I've also seen people cry out for a miracle, but still have to bury their child, I've seen youth fervently pray for restoration in their families, and divorce still happened. Why did this happen? I don't know, but it may be a question you need to process. Will the answers come? Not necessarily, it may lead to more confusion and despair.

But in your moment of asking why, let me guide you with a few thoughts. Jesus said, *"In this world you will have trials and sorrows. But take heart, because I have overcome the world." (John 16:33).* Sometimes we blame God for things that are just a part of life. Jesus recognized we would go through tough and painful situations. We live in a broken world, but Jesus promised He would be with us, and that His Spirit would be our comforter. He defeated death and sin on the cross so that His Spirit could dwell with us and lead us through the trials and sorrows that we must face.

Dear Lord, I don't understand; I don't know why this is happening, but I choose to trust you in this season. I ask that Your Holy Spirit covers me with Your comfort and love. Give me peace in the unknown. I trust you, Amen.

DO YOU HAVE ANY "WHY?" QUESTIONS:

Day 10. In The Why...

*"For my thoughts are not your thoughts,
neither are your ways my ways, declares the Lord."*

(Lord, I recognize that my thoughts and ways may differ from
Your thoughts and ways. I choose to trust you in this season.)

*"For as the heavens are higher than the earth so are my ways higher than
your ways and my thoughts than your thoughts." - Isaiah 55:8-9 ESV.*

(I recognize You are God, You see the future, past, and present.
I trust You with my present circumstances,
even though I may not understand.)

"When you go through deep waters, I will be with you."

(God, I feel like I am treading in deep waters, but I know You are
with me.)

"When you go through rivers of difficulty, you will not drown."

(Thank you for being with me, I trust that you will give me the
strength I need.)

*"When you walk through the fire of oppression, you will not be burned
up; the flames will not consume you." - Isaiah 43:2 NLT*

(Just like You were in the fire with Shadrach, Meshach, and
Abednego, I know You are with me too.
I will not be consumed by depression or oppression,
I give You my sorrow, and ask that You will replace it with joy.)

WHAT WOULD YOU SAY
IF YOU COULD TEXT GOD
RIGHT NOW?

_____

_____

_____

_____

_____

_____

_____

_____

_____

_____

_____

_____

_____

_____

WHAT DO YOU THINK
HE WOULD TEXT BACK?

_____

_____

_____

_____

_____

_____

_____

_____

_____

_____

_____

_____

_____

Day 11. It Wasn't Supposed to be Like This...

"And we know that God causes everything to work together for the good of those who love God and are called according to his purpose for them."
- Romans 8:28 NLT.

Let's look at one of the most iconic deaths in history, the death of Jesus. Now picture this; you have been following this man, Jesus, who you believe to be the Messiah, the Savior of the Jews.
As a Jew, you grew up with a specific ideology of how the Messiah would save your people. Suddenly, your world and ideology are turned upside down as you watch the King of Kings and Lord of Lords hang on the cross. Death comes, and you are shaken to the core;
not only have you lost your friend, but your hero.

Reading the account of Jesus' death, we can often forget his disciples didn't know about resurrection day. On resurrection day, they were sitting and mourning the loss of their friend. I'm sure many of them thought, "It wasn't supposed to be like this." But it was. They didn't understand Jesus was not only saving the Jews but all of humanity. They didn't know that there would be redemption for all in his death and resurrection.

Right now, you may be sitting there like the disciples thinking, "This wasn't supposed to happen! It wasn't supposed to be like this!" The way you envisioned the future has been dismantled.
You may even feel ripped off, and it's okay to feel that way for a short time. Soon, you will have to decide how you will move forward in life. You could allow this situation to cast a shadow on every event in your future or let the Lord heal the hurt and broken expectations.
You can either allow Him to use it for His good or allow it to pull you away from Him. God will use our loss and brokenness for good. He can turn the brokenness into something beautiful.

Dear Jesus, I don't understand why this happened, but I know that you are good and that you are with me. I trust that you will use this situation to bring others closer to you. What the enemy has meant for evil, You will turn it into something beautiful, Amen.

WHAT WOULD YOU LIKE
TO TELL GOD?

Day. 12 Know This

"And we know that God causes everything to work together for the good of those who love God and are called according to his purpose for them."
- Romans 8:28 NLT.

(Lord, I do not see the good in this, but I ask that you use this for your glory. I pray that others will see you and your goodness.)

" For our present troubles are small and won't last very long."

(I know that this deep feeling of grief will not last forever. Thank you for Your healing.)

"Yet they produce for us a glory that vastly outweighs them and will last forever!"

(Lord, as I draw near to You, may Your glory be seen by all who are near me. I pray that this "present trouble" will bring others into a relationship with You.)

"So we don't look at the troubles we can see now; rather, we fix our gaze on things that cannot be seen."

(I choose to focus on you. You understand and see much more than I do. I fix my eyes to seek your grace and peace that is unseen.)

"For the things we see now will soon be gone, but the things we cannot see will last forever." -2 Corinthians 4:17-18 NLT.

(Thank you for the promise of heaven, I trust you, Jesus.)

JESUS, I CHOOSE
TO FOCUS ON:

Day 13. HELP!

"I look up to the mountains—does my help come from there? My help comes from the Lord, who made heaven and earth!" - Psalms 121:1 NLT.

Remember the story in the bible where Peter walked on water? The winds howled, the sea raged, and Peter stepped out of the boat and walked on water like Jesus! However when Peter's attention turned from Jesus he suddenly noticed the storm raging around him, and he began to sink. "Lord save me!" Peter cried out (Matthew 14:30). Jesus reached out and pulled Peter up out of the water, and together they returned to the boat (Matthew 14:30-31).

You may glance over this story and say, "Yeah, yeah, I know, Peter walked on water, I need to have faith, bluh bluh bluh." I ask that you just bear with me for a second and erase all your preconceived ideas about what you think I may say.

As a follower of Jesus, Peter has seen many miracles performed; in fact, he had already been in a boat with Jesus during a storm, remember? The disciples thought they would drown, but then Jesus calmed the storm. Once again, Peter and the disciples are caught in another storm. This time, Peter gets out of the boat to walk on water! This guy has some pretty crazy faith. When Peter panics and begins to sink, Jesus plays the role of a lifeguard and saves him; what's my point? Peter stepped out of the boat in the middle of a storm, began to sink in the middle of the storm, and Jesus rescued him
in the middle of the storm.

Do you think Jesus allowed Peter to sink because he was angry with him? No, he allowed Peter to experience a miracle and saved him when he took his eyes off him. Don't think that because you are in the middle of a storm that God has left you, sometimes we feel that our trials and struggles reflect our worth to God. Jesus is with you in this storm, he hears you, and he will rescue you. Just call for help.

Jesus, sometimes I feel like I am sinking; help me.
I need you; fill me your peace, amen.

JESUS, HELP!
I FEEL:

_____

_____

_____

_____

_____

_____

_____

_____

_____

_____

_____

_____

_____

_____

Day 14. Where Does My Help Come From?

I look up to the mountains- does my help come from there?
(Lord, I recognize that the things of this earth can not heal my heart.)

My help comes from the Lord, who made heaven and earth.
(I recognize my help comes from You, the same God who created heaven and earth.)

He will not let you stumble; the one who watches over you will not slumber.
(Thank you for being with me and keeping me safe.)

Indeed, he who watches over Israel never slumbers or sleeps.
(Lord, just as You have been faithful to Israel, You have been faithful to me.)

The Lord himself watches over you!
(You are with me!)

The Lord stands beside you as your protective shade.
(You are my protector, I rest in Your safety.)

The sun will not harm you by day, nor the moon at night.
(You are with me and protecting me both day and night.)

The Lord keeps you from all harm and watches over your life.
(Lord, thank you for watching over me and protecting me from harm.)

The Lord keeps watch over you as you come and go, both now and forever.
(No matter where I go, I trust that You are with me now and forever.)
Psalm 121:1-8 NLT.

JESUS, WILL YOU SHOW ME WHERE YOU ARE IN THIS SEASON?

Day 15. Stuffing or Healing?

"Trouble and anguish have found me out, but your commandments are my delight."- Psalms 119:143 ESV.

"Grief: deep and poignant distress caused by or as if by bereavement" (Marrian Webster. (n.d.)). The definition of grief describes inner turmoil well, poignant distress. Everyone deals with grief or loss differently, but regardless, everyone must walk through a process of resolving the poignant distress. Are you allowing yourself to grieve, or are you "stuffing" those feelings?

"Well, what do you mean?" you may ask. Often when someone is walking through a loss, they either; allow themselves to ride the rollercoaster of emotions, or they shut down, distract themselves, and try to move on. Which one are you doing? Are you allowing yourself to grieve?

The journey through this valley can be filled with ups and downs, turns, and plummets. You will have moments where you feel sad, moments where you feel angry, and moments where you feel okay. And that's all okay; whatever you feel, allow yourself to work through those feelings.

Sometimes as Christians, we can think, "Well, I shouldn't be sad or mad because God is with me. If I feel angry or depressed, I'm not trusting God," but this is not always the case. Yes, God is with you; he is for you, he promises to turn your sadness into joy, and he will work all things together for good. However, God created us to feel, and he knows that grief is a process of healing. He doesn't expect you to lose something and just be okay. Remember, Jesus promised to be our comforter.Whatever you are feeling, it's okay; allow yourself
to feel, grieve, and let the Lord walk with you as you heal.

*Dear Lord, I recognize that I must allow myself to deal with my feelings and emotions. Thank you for your grace as
I navigate through this valley, amen.*

ARE YOU STUFFING OR HEALING?

WHAT WOULD YOU LIKE
GOD TO KNOW?

Day 16. Wandering in Grief

"For you are God, my only safe haven."
(God, you are my safe place.)

"Why have you tossed me aside?"
(Honestly, sometimes I wonder where You are,
or if You have abandoned me.)

"Why must I wander around in grief, oppressed by my enemies?"

(I wonder why I have to walk through this grief.)

" Send out your light and your truth; let them guide me."

(Lord, I need you to guide me, show me Your truth.)

"Let them lead me to your holy mountain, to the place where you live."

(As I seek You and allow You to lead me, I will find rest in Your
presence.)

"There I will go to the altar of God, to God—the source of all my joy."
(As I worship You, You will fill me with joy.)

"I will praise you with my harp, O God, my God!" -Psalm 43:2-4 NLT.
(God, You are my God and worthy to be praised!)

WHAT COULD THE BENEFITS OF GRIEF BE? WHAT HAS THIS LOSS MADE YOU REFLECT ON?

Day 17. Is God Good?

"For I know the plans I have for you, declares the Lord,
plans to prosper you and not to harm you, plans to give you
a hope and a future." - Jeremiah 29:11 NIV.

Jeremiah 29:11 is one of those scriptures that everyone memorizes. You have probably seen it or have heard it before. It's easy to feel like God is good when life is full of beautiful moments. However, when life is hard, a loved one has died, or a parent has walked out, one may question, "where is God? Why did He let this happen?"

I have encountered many people who ask these questions, and honestly, I have asked these same questions myself. If you look at Jeremiah 29:11 in the full context, the prophet Jeremiah was delivering a word from the Lord to the nation of Israel, whom Babylon had captured. The Israelites had been so far away from God that some scholars believe they were committing child sacrifices to idols. God allows the Babylons to invade, and guess what? The Israelites remember God and turn their focus back to him.

Why was it so crucial for the Israelites to turn back to God? Because they were the chosen bloodline for Jesus to enter the world. The plan was Jesus, the hope was Jesus, and the future was Jesus. Without Jesus, there would not be salvation, and because of Jesus, we get to have a personal relationship with the Father. Bad things happen because we still live in a world filled with sin, death, and human error. However, God made a way for us to receive his love and peace. Jesus said, "Here on earth you will have many trials and sorrows. But take heart, because I have overcome the world." (John 16:33). My conclusion; Yes, God is still good, and the results of a sinful world do not define his goodness. His goodness is defined by his promise to never leave or forsake you.

God, I believe You are a good Father; thank you for never leaving me or forsaking me. I trust You in this valley, amen.

WHERE CAN YOU SEE THE GOODNESS OF GOD IN YOUR LIFE RIGHT NOW?

_____

_____

_____

_____

_____

_____

_____

_____

_____

_____

_____

_____

_____

_____

Day 18. God is Good.

"Give thanks to the Lord, for he is good!"
(Lord, Thank you for Your goodness; you are a good God!"

"His faithful love endures forever."
(Thank you for your faithful love that lasts forever.)

"Give thanks to the God of gods."
(Thank you for being a God who is personal,
Thank you for caring for me.)

"His faithful love endures forever."
(I know that You have not rejected me, You will love me forever.)

"Give thanks to the Lord of lords."
(Thank you for being a just and sovereign Lord.)

"His faithful love endures forever."
(I believe you love me and will never stop loving me.)

"Give thanks to him who alone does mighty miracles."
(Thank you, Lord, for the miracles that you have done in my life.)

"His faithful love endures forever." - *Psalms 136:1-5 NLT.*
(You really love me, no matter what I have done.)

IF YOU COULD TEXT GOD RIGHT NOW, WHAT WOULD YOU TEXT HIM?

HOW DO YOU THINK
HE WOULD RESPOND?

_____

_____

_____

_____

_____

_____

_____

_____

_____

_____

_____

_____

_____

Day 19. The Depth of Despair

"Why are you cast down, O my soul, and why are you in turmoil within me? Hope in God; for I shall again praise him, my salvation and my God."
- Psalm 43:5 ESV.

The definition of despair is this: "the feeling of no longer having any hope." (Britannica.) As you walk through the valley of loss, you will have to sort through many feelings and emotions. Many of your emotions are valid, but the enemy would love to pull you into a pit of despair if you don't guard your heart. Why? Because the enemy plans to keep you as far away from Jesus as possible.

"The thief comes only to steal and kill and destroy. I came that they may have life and have it abundantly." (John 10:10). Despair is a lack of hope, and Jesus is our hope. Our hope is not in material things or even in things going perfectly as planned. Jesus defeated death and overcame the possibility of eternal separation from God.
Our hope is in heaven.

If you feel yourself losing hope, press into Jesus and the promises in the word of God. Do not let despair sink in, do not lose sight of your hope. "And I am convinced that nothing can ever separate us from God's love. Neither death nor life, neither angels nor demons, neither our fears for today nor our worries about tomorrow—not even the powers of hell can separate us from God's love." (Romans 8:38). Loss is not the end, and this is not the end of your story. May the God of peace fill you with hope.

Jesus, I give you my despair; I don't want anything to do with it. I am sad and disappointed, but I refuse to allow the enemy to fill my heart with despair. Jesus, I ask that you will replace any despair with hope; amen.

JESUS, I FEEL...

Day 20. Your Promises

"He will wipe every tear from their eyes, and there will be no more death or sorrow or crying or pain. All these things are gone forever."
- Revelation 21:4 NLT.

(Jesus, thank you for the promise of Heaven. Thank you that one day there will be no more grief. Thank you for promising to be my comforter.)

"And I am convinced that nothing can ever separate us from God's love."

(I believe the truth in your word and that nothing can separate me from your love.)

"Neither death nor life, neither angels nor demons, neither our fears for today nor our worries about tomorrow—not even the powers of hell can separate us from God's love." - Romans 8:38 NLT.

(Thank you, Jesus, that You are with me and that nothing can separate me from your love. I give You my fear, my worries and I throw away any lies that tell me there is no hope.)

ARE THERE ANY NEGATIVE THOUGHTS YOU ARE STRUGGLING WITH?

WHAT ARE SOME BIBLICAL TRUTHS YOU CAN REPLACE THEM WITH?

_____

_____

_____

_____

_____

_____

_____

_____

_____

_____

_____

_____

_____

_____

PART 2:
ANGER, DEPRESSION
AND DENIAL

Day 21. So Angry

"But you, O Lord, are a God of compassion and mercy, slow to get angry and filled with unfailing love and faithfulness." - Psalm 86:15 NLT.

Anger... if you haven't already had a moment where you feel that burning sensation of anger, I hate to break it to you, but you will probably experience it at some point on your journey through loss. Despite what preconceived ideas you may have about anger, let me tell you something, it's okay to feel angry.

"What? It's okay if I feel angry?" Yes, it is. Feeling angry is not a sin, but what you do with that anger can be a sin. The apostle Paul said it best, "And 'don't sin by letting anger control you.' Don't let the sun go down while you are still angry, for anger gives a foothold to the devil." (Ephesians 4:26-27). Sometimes in anger, humans have poor responses; they act out, hurt others, and get themselves into trouble.

The feeling of anger isn't the problem; it's how one reacts. Now, I am not saying that you should walk around angry. If anger is not dealt with it can fester into other problems, and as Paul said, it will open you up to allow the enemy to root himself into your life.

So, what should you do with anger? First, you need to recognize the root emotions that are causing anger to well up. Anger is often a response to other feelings or emotions, like anxiety, guilt, sadness, rejection, or feeling a lack of feeling safe. If you are angry, take some time to figure out the root emotion triggering your anger. Whatever it is, entrust those feelings to the Lord, he already knows how you feel, and if you allow him to, he will help you heal the brokenness.

Dear Lord, help me recognize what is causing me to feel angry; I don't want to feel like this anymore. I need Your peace, and I need Your Spirit to show me how to heal; amen.

IF YOU COULD TEXT GOD RIGHT NOW, WHAT WOULD YOU TEXT HIM?

_____

_____

_____

_____

_____

_____

_____

_____

_____

_____

_____

_____

_____

_____

_____

Day 22. In Peace

"Don't sin by letting anger control you."
(Lord, I give you my anger, I refuse to let it control me.)

Think about it overnight and remain silent.
(Help me to think before I act out in anger and stay quiet
when my words may be hurtful.)

Offer sacrifices in the right spirit, and trust the Lord.
(In everything I do, I want my heart to be in the right place,
I trust you, Lord.)

"Many people say, "Who will show us better times?"
(Right now, things are tough, and I wish things were like
they used to be.)

Let your face smile on us, Lord.
(Lord, may this new season be filled with Your favor.)

*"You have given me greater joy than those who have abundant
harvests of grain and new wine."*
(I know that You are my source of joy, nothing in this world
can fulfill my soul.)

*"In peace I will lie down and sleep, for you alone,
O Lord, will keep me safe." - Psalms 4:4-8 NLT.*
(I give you my worry, anxiety, and anger, I will lie down
and sleep in peace, for You are with me.)

LORD, I NEED...

Day 23. They Mean Well, But...

"Always be humble and gentle. Be patient with each other, making allowance for each other's faults because of your love." - Ephesians 4:2 NLT.

Loss is a very vulnerable time, and your emotions are probably running all over the place. You may feel like your heart has been cut out of your chest and is just lying in the open for all to see. In this state of vulnerability, the people around you may unintentionally say something downright hurtful or unnecessary. Which is then brushed off with "Well, they meant well," or "Oh, don't take it so seriously." yeah, it happens. Unfortunately, sometimes people say or do the wrong thing, and it can really hurt.

Why are people so insensitive? Sometimes it may be because they don't quite understand what you are experiencing or are unsure of how to respond, so they react in a way that comes across as insensitive. So, what can you do about it?

Guard your heart. Your focus right now needs to be on protecting your heart from anger. What does that look like? Does that mean telling everyone off? No, If the unwanted comment came from a close friend or family member, talk with them about it and resolve the hurt. Otherwise, remember that most people mean well but may not understand what you are going through. Accept the good advice or sympathy and let go of the rest. Give unwanted comments to Jesus, forgive those who were hurtful, and forgive. Remember to give your fellow humans grace, just as I hope others will give you grace as you walk through this season. Humans are human, and they will make mistakes. In this season, walk humbly and be quick to forgive, even if they may not deserve it.

Jesus, I need an extra portion of grace in this season. I forgive those who have been hurtful, and I give You the hurt and ask that You will replace it with peace. Help me walk in humility and gentleness, amen.

LORD, I FORGIVE...

_____

_____

_____

_____

_____

_____

_____

_____

_____

_____

_____

_____

_____

_____

Day 24. My Fill of Fruit.

" But the Holy Spirit produces this kind of fruit in our lives: love, joy, peace, patience, kindness, goodness, faithfulness, gentleness, and self-control."

(Lord, in this season, I want the fruit of the Spirit to be evident in my life.)

(Fill me with:
- Love for those who need to be loved.
- Joy where there is sadness.
- Peace in the storm.
- Patience for my family.
- Kindness for others, even if they have not been kind to me.
- Self-control for those that are hard to deal with.
- Gentleness in the way I speak to others.
- I pray that those around me will see Your goodness and faithfulness in my life.)

"There is no law against these things!" - Galatians 5:22-23

(I am thankful that even in the valley of loss, the Holy Spirit is still working, I declare in Jesus' name that those around me will see His fruit in my life.)

TELL THE LORD WHAT'S ON YOUR MIND.

Day. 25 A Bitter Taste

"Get rid of all bitterness, rage, anger, harsh words, and slander, as well as all types of evil behavior." Ephesians 4:31 NLT.

Think about a famous fairytale you may have read or watched. Got it? Now think about the villain. Perhaps they were; a grumpy old witch, an evil lady who lusted after youth and beauty, or maybe a vain and pompous soldier. Have you ever wondered how those villains became so hateful? If you were to analyze any fairytale villains, I bet deep down, they all have a root of bitterness in their hearts.

Bitterness is an awful feeling, any seed of anger that has been allowed to cultivate will grow into bitterness, and bitterness is much harder to uproot once it has dug down deep into one's heart.
Like Paul said, "Get rid of bitterness" (Eph 4:31).
Do not allow it to grow. It is an unwanted weed growing in the garden of your heart.

The enemy would love to cultivate a root of bitterness in your life right about now. Guard your heart as you walk through this season of grief, do not allow bitterness to grow in your heart toward others or the Lord. Forgive those who have hurt you, even if you feel they don't deserve it. If it is God with whom you are angry, bring that anger to him. The Lord already knows how you feel, and he is waiting to walk through this with you.

Jesus, I want nothing to do with bitterness. I do not want it to have any place in my life. I give you my heart and repent for allowing any bitterness to grow. I forgive those who have let me down. Fill my heart with Your peace, amen.

IF YOU COULD WRITE GOD A NOTE, WHAT WOULD YOU WRITE?

_____

_____

_____

_____

_____

_____

_____

_____

_____

_____

_____

_____

_____

_____

Day 26. Walking in Grace.

"Always be humble and gentle."

(Lord, help me to walk in humility and to communicate with gentleness.)

" Be patient with each other, making allowance for each other's faults because of your love.

(Help me to be patient with those around me, help me to give grace to those who may not deserve it.)

"Make every effort to keep yourselves united in the Spirit, binding yourselves together with peace." - Ephesians 4:2-3 NLT.

(Give me the wisdom to know how to fight for unity with my family and friends, Lord fill each one of us with Your peace.)

"Get rid of all bitterness, rage, anger, harsh words, and slander, as well as all types of evil behavior." - Ephesians 4:31 NLT.

(I want nothing to do with the spirit of bitterness, rage, anger, harsh words, or slander. Jesus, clean my heart from anything that may be trying to take root.)

JESUS, I NEED YOU, I GIVE YOU MY...

Day 27: All Alone

"I will not leave you orphans; I will come to you." - John 14:18 ESV.

Grief has a way of making one feel alone. That moment when you see the empty spot at the table or go to send a text that will never be replied to, it hits - the gut-wrenching feeling of loneliness. Loneliness because you miss someone, and perhaps because you feel like you're still stuck in a place of grief all alone. It's strange to be in a room of people or surrounded by loved ones, yet still feel a sense of loneliness. When the loss primarily impacts you and your immediate family, it may seem like others have already moved on while you are still here, working through the grief.

The truth is, many of your friends probably have moved on from focusing on your loss. But that doesn't mean they have abandoned you in your grief. Always remember that your friends and family care for you. I bet they are willing to hear what is going on in your thoughts, even if they have moved forward in their journey with grief. They may just need to be reminded that you are still grieving. The people around you can't fix your broken heart for you; only Jesus can do that.

Jesus promised that he would never leave you or forsake you. In John 14:18, Jesus promised that he would not leave you orphaned but that he would send the Holy Spirit. The Holy Spirit is our Comforter (John 14:26 KJV). Stand on His promises, you have not been abandoned, and you are not alone. When the loneliness feels like it may be too much to bear, spend some time focusing on His presence.

Jesus, I rebuke the lie that I am abandoned and alone in my grief. Thank you for your Holy Spirit and those you have placed in my life as support. I trust you to heal my heart, amen.

IF YOU COULD TEXT GOD RIGHT NOW, WHAT WOULD YOU SAY?

_____

_____

_____

_____

_____

_____

_____

_____

_____

_____

_____

_____

_____

_____

Day 28. Never Alone

"You go before me and follow me."
(Thank you for surrounding me with your presence.)

" You place your hand of blessing on my head."
(Thank you for placing your hand of blessing on my head.)

"Such knowledge is too wonderful for me, too great for me to understand!"
(I can't even begin to understand how great you are!)

"I can never escape from your Spirit!"
(No matter where I go, Your Spirit knows where I am)

"I can never get away from your presence!"
(Thank you for not leaving me an orphan and that the presence of the Holy Spirit is with me always.)

"If I go up to heaven, you are there; if I go down to the grave, you are there."
(You are with me in the good, and you are with me even in loss and grief, You are a good Father.)

"If I ride the wings of the morning, if I dwell by the farthest oceans, even there your hand will guide me, and your strength will support me."
- Psalms 139:5-10 NLT
(Thank you for being with me no matter where I go. You are my guide, my strength, and my support.)

GOD, I FEEL...

_____

_____

_____

_____

_____

_____

_____

_____

_____

_____

_____

_____

_____

_____

_____

_____

Day 29. Not Today Satan

"For we are not fighting against flesh-and-blood enemies, but against evil rulers and authorities of the unseen world, against mighty powers in this dark world, and against evil spirits in the heavenly places."
- Ephesians 6:12 NLT.

God is real, and so is our enemy Satan. His plan is simple; to keep as many of God's creations from Him. Satan's plan for you is destruction, and he will try and achieve that by convincing you of a few things.

He will try to convince you that God is not good, he will try to convince you that you are not worthy, and he will try and convince you that you have no authority over him. Satan's battlefield is the mind. That despair and fear trying to seep in, those dark and negative thoughts, are all schemes and lies from the pit of hell. These lies are not your inheritance. As a child of God, your inheritance is to live life abundantly; spiritually, physically, and mentally.

So what can one do when in the thick of an internal battle? Fight. The word of God is your weapon; use it. When those dark thoughts come, shoot them down with truth. When you have those thoughts that tell you that you are worthless, take that thought captive like this; " I reject the lie that I am worthless and unloved. I replace it with truth; I am loved, I am a child of God, and I am worthy because Jesus died for me."

Lastly, do not stay silent if you are struggling with depression or dark thoughts. The enemy wants to isolate you, and one soldier is easier to beat than two. When you share your struggles with trustworthy people, your burden will become lighter, they can help you find professional help if needed, and there is no shame in needing someone to help you in this battle.

Dear Jesus, I recognize that you have given me authority over Satan; I rebuke the lies I have believed. I am worthy, I am loved, and I am needed, amen.

WHO DOES GOD SAY YOU ARE? WHO HAS HE CREATED YOU TO BE?

_____

_____

_____

_____

_____

_____

_____

_____

_____

_____

_____

_____

_____

_____

_____

_____

Day 30 Weapons of Warfare

"Stand your ground, putting on the belt of truth and the body armor of God's righteousness."

(Lord, I stand firm in the truth that You are God, and I guard my heart with Your righteousness.)

"For shoes, put on the peace that comes from the Good News so that you will be fully prepared."

(Jesus, You are the Good News, I walk in the peace and knowledge that you are with me.)

" In addition to all of these, hold up the shield of faith to stop the fiery arrows of the devil."

(God, I believe in You, You are a good Father, I will not accept the lies of the devil.)

" Put on salvation as your helmet, and take the sword of the Spirit, which is the word of God." - Ephesians 6:14-17 NLT.

(I know that I am saved by the blood of Jesus and by His grace alone. Lord, teach me to use the scriptures to fight my battles.)

GOD, I WANT YOU TO KNOW...

Day 31. Grace upon Grace

"But he said to me, "My grace is sufficient for you, for my power is made perfect in weakness." Therefore I will boast all the more gladly of my weaknesses, so that the power of Christ may rest upon me." 2 Corinthians 12:9 ESV.

Many people walking through a loss or tragedy will often describe a sensation of grace that is almost unexplainable. Like a cloud passing over the blazing sun, providing a sense of relief from the burning heat. God's grace is sufficient. He covers His children with His grace, just as He provided fire by night and a cloud by day for the Israelites as they fled from Egypt (Exodus 13:21)

As you walk through this valley, remember that God's grace is sufficient for you. In your grief and weakness, He is near. Through the expression of His grace, those around you will see God's goodness. If you feel like God is not close, take a moment to observe His covering of grace actively. The peace you have had in those painful moments, or perhaps that calmness you felt as you made some tough decision; that is what God's grace feels like. It's not an absence of sadness but may be best described as an added sense of peace or an unexplainable ability to endure the unimaginable.

Just as God has extended His grace to cover you, remember to have a little extra grace to those around you. It is challenging to navigate through grief, and people may say or do things that seem unhelpful or perhaps insensitive. Remember, If God's grace is sufficient for you, you can also have sufficient grace for those around you.

Dear Lord, Thank you for Your covering of grace. I need You now more than ever. As I begin to allow my heart to heal, I pray that I will feel and see
Your grace upon my life. Jesus, help me be an example of Your grace to those around me, amen.

WHERE HAVE YOU SEEN GOD'S GRACE IN THIS SEASON?

Day 32. Sufficient

"But he said to me, 'My grace is sufficient for you, for my power is made perfect in weakness.'"

(Lord, Your grace is enough to get me through this. I pray that in my weakness, others will see Your power and love.)

"Therefore I will boast all the more gladly of my weaknesses, so that the power of Christ may rest upon me."

(I pray that in this valley, those around me will witness Your power and that they will know that You are God!)

"For the sake of Christ, then, I am content with weaknesses, insults, hardships, persecutions, and calamities. For when I am weak, then I am strong." - 2 Corinthians 12:9-10 ESV.

(No matter what comes my way, I pray that my weakness, hardships, ridicule, persecution, or tragedies will be used to bring You glory.
Because of You, in my weakness, I am strong.)

GOD, THANK YOU FOR:

Day 33. Healer

"When they call on me, I will answer; I will be with them in trouble. I will rescue and honor them." - Psalms 91:15 NLT.

Right now, wading through the grief may feel like trudging through thick mud. At this point, many people in your life have probably diverted their attention from your loss to other situations in life, as they should. But here you are, still walking through it, feeling the heavy weight of the loss.

Some would say that "time heals all wounds," I disagree with this statement. Although time does put distance between your present situation and the moment of raw emotions associated with loss. Healing comes when we allow one's heart to heal from the wounds, and Jesus is the ultimate healer.

If a tornado whipped through a house, it would be safe to assume that it would take some time to put it back in order. Time itself does not do the work; you physically have to sort through the mess to bring restoration and order back. Wounds are healed when one takes the time to sort through the messy emotions to heal the wounds.

Some people never allow themselves to sort through their grief; they shove it down, sit in the loss, and never move on. That, my friend, is not the Lord's plan for you. He wants to help you heal your heart. Do not let this loss rob you of your life; do not let depression linger forever. You must heal because there is still a beautiful life to live. Just start by picking up one piece at a time and giving it to the One who can heal all wounds.

Jesus, help me rebuild "my house" and sort through my grief. You are my healer. I give you my heart and trust that you will heal it, amen.

IF YOU COULD SEND GOD A TEXT, WHAT WOULD YOU TEXT:

HOW WOULD HE RESPOND?

Day 34. My Refuge

"Those who live in the shelter of the Most High will find rest in the shadow of the Almighty.

(Lord, You are my shelter, my soul finds rest in Your presence.)

"This I declare about the Lord: He alone is my refuge, my place of safety; he is my God, and I trust him."

(You are my refuge and my safe place, I trust You.)

"For he will rescue you from every trap   and protect you from deadly disease."

(You are my rescuer and protector.)

"He will cover you with his feathers."

(I am safe, I rest in Your presence.)

"He will shelter you with his wings."

(Like a mother hen protects her chicks under her wings, you are my protector)

"His faithful promises are your armor and protection." - Psalms 91:1-4 NLT.

(I know You are faithful. You are a God who keeps His promises.)

LORD, I WANT TO TELL YOU...

Day 35. Fight For Peace

"But the time is coming—indeed it's here now—when you will be scattered, each one going his own way, leaving me alone. Yet I am not alone because the Father is with me. I have told you all this so that you may have peace in me. Here on earth you will have many trials and sorrows. But take heart, because I have overcome the world." - John 16:32-33 NLT.

When your days are filled with the heaviness of loss and moments of sifting through questions and broken dreams, it can be hard to maintain peace within your soul. Those feelings of turmoil and distress may turn like a dryer during the spin cycle. You go to bed spinning and wake up spinning. How do you make the cycle stop? When your life seems to be falling apart, fight for peace. Fight for your soul to be at rest. Fight for your mind to be quiet and your heart to be confident that the Lord is with you. Jesus is the Prince of Peace; when you rest in Him, you will find peace, regardless of your circumstances.

The enemy would love to keep you in a cycle of distress and turmoil, but no matter what "trial or sorrows" (John 16:33) you walk through, remind yourself; that Jesus has overcome every single one of them. He died for you so that you could receive your inheritance of peace. Take a moment to quiet your heart before the Lord and seek His peace each day. Fight for it, do not let Satan steal your peace.

Jesus, I recognize that You are the Prince of Peace. I receive Your peace. I replace all turmoil, distress, and anxiousness with peace. Jesus, teach me how to fight for peace, amen.

WHAT SITUATION ARE YOU ALLOWING TO STEAL YOUR PEACE?

ASK JESUS TO HELP YOU FIND PEACE.

Day 36. The Gift of Peace.

"But when the Father sends the Advocate as my representative—that is, the Holy Spirit—he will teach you everything and will remind you of everything I have told you."

(Lord, thank you for sending the Holy Spirit as my advocate and counselor. Holy Spirit, teach me to rely on You and help me to remember Your Promises.)

"I am leaving you with a gift—peace of mind and heart."

(I receive your gift of peace. Both for my mind and in my heart. I am done allowing stress and anxiousness to rule my heart and mind.)

"And the peace I give is a gift the world cannot give.
So don't be troubled or afraid."
- John 14:26-27 NLT.

(Forgive me for looking to the things of this world to bring me peace. I need Your gift of peace. Jesus, I ask that you will replace all of my fear and worries with Your peace.)

WHAT ARE SOME THOUGHTS
OR FEELINGS THAT YOU NEED
TO TRADE IN FOR PEACE?
ASK THE LORD TO REPLACE
THEM WITH PEACE.

Day 37. Sounds Mind

"For God has not given us a spirit of fear, but of power and of love and of a sound mind." - 2 Timothy 1:7 NKJV.

A sound mind? What does that mean? I would describe a person with a sound mind as someone who is: thinking and interpreting situations clearly, acting reasonably and rationally, and not allowing one's mind to be dictated by emotions. 2 Timothy 1:7 says that "God has not given us a spirit of fear but of power and love and of a sound mind." You were created to have a sound mind.

In his cunning way, Satan will often take advantage of the valley of grief, planting seeds of confusion and attempting to fill your mind with fear and anxiety. Reject those lies and the fear that may try to creep in. Fight for clarity and protect your mind with the truth. You are loved, you are free, you are a child of God, and your Father has good plans for you! God created your spirit to be filled with power, love, and a sound mind.

In 2 Timothy 1:7, some bible translations (like the ESV) have translated the phrase "sound mind" to "self-control." While they may seem like two very different phrases, I would argue that together they reveal the key to maintaining a sound mind. A sound mind is established when you keep control over what thoughts you allow yourself to believe. Now is the time to discipline yourself to dig deeper into the scriptures and fight for soundness of mind. Fight to throw out any negative thoughts that come into your mind.

Lord, you have given me a spirit of power, love, and a sound mind. I receive that inheritance. I rebuke all fear, anxiety, and confusion that the enemy may be trying to plant, amen.

LORD, I FEEL...

Day 38. Seeking Peace

"You will keep in perfect peace all who trust in you, all whose thoughts are fixed on you!"

(Lord, I trust You, I turn my attention towards You. Thank you for Your perfect peace.)

"Trust in the Lord always, for the Lord God is the eternal Rock.
- Isaiah 26:3-4 NLT.

(I can trust in You because You are forever stable, You are my rock.)

"Lord, we show our trust in you by obeying your laws;
our heart's desire is to glorify your name."

(My heart desires to glorify You, help me to honor Your laws, and walk in obedience.)

"In the night I search for you; in the morning I earnestly seek you."
- Isaiah 26: 8-9 NLT.

(I am so thankful that You do not hide from Your people and that You promised that those who seek You, I will find You.)

IF YOU COULD TEXT GOD RIGHT NOW, WHAT WOULD YOU TEXT HIM?

_____

_____

_____

_____

_____

_____

_____

_____

_____

_____

_____

_____

_____

_____

Day 39. This Is How We Fight the Battles

"Always be joyful. Never stop praying. Be thankful in all circumstances, for this is God's will for you who belong to Christ Jesus."
- 1 Thessalonians 5:16-18 NLT.

When you feel the war raging within your soul, and your world seems to be spinning out of control, remember, a war is raging in the spiritual realm as well, and all of heaven is on your side. Satan wants you for himself; he will try to bring lies and confusion into your heart, just like he did to Eve in the very beginning. Now is the time to press in, rise, and fight back.

Fight back with unceasing joy, endless prayers, and thankfulness (1Thessalonians 5:16-18). If you feel yourself losing ground in the battle, find your joy again. Joy is not just an outward appearance of happiness; joy is a deep-rooted sense of contentment, which comes from an overflow of knowing the Father's love. When the battle rages, focus on His love for you. Turn that worship music on and soak in the love of God.

Never stop praying; prayer is a potent weapon against the enemy. You are a child of the living God, and He has given you authority. When you pray, mountains can move, and demons will tremble. Use your voice and pray out the scriptures. When you turn your heart to prayer, you turn your focus from yourself and your attention to the Lord.

In every circumstance, give thanks; nothing drives out depression and heaviness like a thankful heart. When you feel like depression is sinking in, pause and begin to focus on something you are thankful for.

Jesus, thank you for being with me in the battle. Show me how to find joy, turn to prayer, and walk in thanksgiving, amen. I turn to You.

I AM THANKFUL FOR...

Day 40. The Lord Is My Strength

"In your strength I can crush an army; with my God I can scale any wall."

(Lord, you are my strength, I can fight this battle and overcome them because You are with me.)

"God's way is perfect."

(I trust Your ways and the plans You have for me.)

"All the Lord's promises prove true."
(You are faithful to fulfill Your promises.)

"He is a shield for all who look to him for protection."

(Lord, I need You, thank you for Your protection.)

"For who is God except the Lord?"

(You are God, there is no other God except You!)

" Who but our God is a solid rock?"

(You are my safe place, I trust You.)

"God arms me with strength, and he makes my way perfect."
Psalm 18:29-32 NLT.

(Thank you for giving me strength to fight, I trust in Your perfect ways.)

I FEEL LIKE
I AM FIGHTING AGAINST...

_____

_____

_____

_____

_____

_____

_____

LORD, I NEED...

_____

_____

_____

_____

_____

_____

_____

Day 41. Fear Not

"The Lord is my light and my salvation- so why should I be afraid? The Lord is my fortress, protecting me from danger, so why should I tremble?"
- Psalm 27:1 NLT.

A variation of the phrase "Do not be afraid" was written 365 times throughout the Bible; I think the Lord was trying to make a point. Fear is not a part of a believer's inheritance, but it is one of Satan's tricky tactics to get you under his control.

Grief can be a prime opportunity for fear to walk into one's life. The voice of fear often sounds like this: "What if (fill in the blank) happens?" or "What if I can't (fill in the blank)?" Notice the trend, "what if". The enemy will use that "what if" to bring that paralyzing fear, and that fear can keep you from living the life that God has created you to live.

My friend, the Lord has not called you to live a life dictated by the fear of the "what if?" He has called you to live a life in boldness and confidence. Confidence that no matter what happens, the Lord will be with you. If you go and seek out those 365 verses that contain the phrase "Do not be afraid," you will find it is often accompanied by a statement like, "The Lord is with you." My friend, The God who created the universe is with you! Do not be afraid; when disaster strikes, the Lord will give you the grace to overcome. He is with you.

Lord, thank you for Your faithfulness; I give You my fear. I refuse to listen to the voice of fear. I choose to trust in Your world and believe that You are with me. Teach me Your ways, teach me to trust You, amen.

LORD, RIGHT NOW,
I AM AFRAID THAT...

_____

_____

_____

_____

_____

_____

_____

_____

_____

_____

_____

_____

_____

_____

LORD, I CHOOSE TO TRUST YOU WITH...

Day 42. The Lord is With Me

"The Lord is my light and my salvation— so why should I be afraid?"

(You are my light in the darkness and my salvation,
I will not be afraid.)

"The Lord is my fortress, protecting me from danger, so why should I tremble?"

(You are my safe place, Lord, I give you my fear.)

*"When evil people come to devour me, when my enemies
and foes attack me they will stumble and fall."*

(Lord, You are my protector, You will keep me safe from my enemies.)

"Though a mighty army surrounds me, my heart will not be afraid."

(Even in the midst of the battle, I will not be afraid because You are
with me.)

"Even if I am attacked, I will remain confident." - Psalm 27:1-3 NLT.

(I am confident that You are with me!)

LORD, I WANT YOU TO KNOW...

Day 43. Restore

"He restores my soul. He leads me in paths of righteousness for his name's sake." - Psalms 23:3 ESV.

Grief is like a wrecking ball, violently swinging and shattering everything in its path. When loss comes, everything changes; Families are broken, hopes and dreams are destroyed, often within seconds. Grief leaves many broken pieces in its wake, but there is good news, God is a God of restoration. He will restore your soul.

God longs to help you pick up the broken pieces and fashion something new. It may be hard to imagine a life outside of loss and grief, and that's okay; just take it one day at a time. No, it won't be the same as before, and it's okay to grieve the loss of those broken hopes and dreams. However, something new must come, the past is the past, and there is so much to look forward to in the future. As new hopes and dreams emerge from the brokenness, the spark of excitement for what is to come will return.

As you wait, fix your eyes upon the restorer, Jesus, and watch what He will do. Trust that He is with you, guiding your path out of the valley and toward a new adventure. It may be messy, perhaps a little sad, but a new adventure is coming, and that is exciting. As the saying goes, "Rome wasn't built in a day," so remember to be patient with yourself, patient with others, and patient with the Lord; wait on Him, and he will restore your soul.

Dear Jesus, Thank you for being the great restorer. I give you the broken pieces of my heart. Thank you for the healing that has already taken place and for the healing to come, amen.

WHAT IS GOING ON IN YOUR HEART RIGHT NOW? TELL THE LORD WHAT'S ON YOUR MIND.

Day 44. He Heals the Brokenhearted

"The Spirit of the Lord God is upon me, because the Lord has anointed me
to bring good news to the poor;"

(Thank you for sending Your Holy Spirit and the good news of salvation through Jesus.)

"he has sent me to bind up the brokenhearted,"

(Thank you for healing my broken heart)

"to proclaim liberty to the captives, and the opening of the prison to those who are bound;"

(Thank you for freeing me from the enemy's schemes; I am free because You have redeemed me from my sin.)

"to proclaim the year of the Lord's favor, and the day of vengeance of our God;"

(Your favor is with me, and Your justice will reign.)

"to comfort all who mourn;"- Isaiah 61:1-2 ESV.

(Thank you for Your comfort.)

DEAR JESUS,
MY HEART FEELS...

Day 45. Living Hope

"Blessed be the God and Father of our Lord Jesus Christ! According to his great mercy, he has caused us to be born again to a living hope through the resurrection of Jesus Christ from the dead, to an inheritance that is imperishable, undefiled, and unfading, kept in heaven for you," - 1 Peter 1:3-4 NLT.

Hope: a "desire accompanied by expectation of or belief in fulfillment." (Marian Webster Dictionary). A Loss can bring a lot of confusion; suddenly, your life has changed, and a new life must be planned. Your expectations have been crushed, and you may feel as though you were robbed of your future hopes and dreams. However, those who believe that Jesus Christ is Lord have hope beyond that which earthly hope can offer. Theirs is a Living Hope.

When Jesus rose from the grave, He defeated death and gave us all the "right to become children of God." (John 1:12). When you receive the gift of salvation, you get the promise of heaven, and nothing in this world can take that away from you! Jesus is your Living Hope, the fulfillment of all of God's promises, and the bridge between you and the Father. Regardless of what may come in this life, you can have this hope; God is with you, God is for you, and heaven is your eternal prize. This hope is "imperishable, undefiled, and unfading," (1 Peter 1:4).

One day you will stand before the Lord, and there will be no more tears or sorrow, no more suffering or death (Revelation 21:4). What a day that will be; not only will we see our loved ones, but we will set our eyes on Jesus, the perfect sacrifices, and our Living Hope.

Jesus, thank you for what you did for me on the cross. I love you and place my hope and trust in you, amen.

WRITE A NOTE TO JESUS. WHAT DO YOU WANT HIM TO KNOW?

Day 46. Jesus is my Living Hope

"Blessed be the God and Father of our Lord Jesus Christ!"

(Father, You are holy, there is none like You!)

"According to his great mercy, he has caused us to be born again to a living hope through the resurrection of Jesus Christ from the dead,"

(I am in awe of the sacrifice You made for me, You gave Your one and only Son to die for me. He is my Living Hope!)

" to an inheritance that is imperishable, undefiled, and unfading, kept in heaven for you,"

(I recognize that through Jesus's death and resurrection, I gain the inheritance of eternal life, which is imperishable, undefiled, and unfading.)

"who by God's power are being guarded through faith for a salvation ready to be revealed in the last time." - 1 Peter 1: 3-5 ESV.

(Thank you, Father, for making a way for me to dwell with You in Your house forever!)

IF YOU COULD ASK GOD ANYTHING, WHAT WOULD YOU ASK HIM?

Day 47. God in the Chaos

"And he said, "Go out and stand on the mount before the Lord."
And behold, the Lord passed by, and a great and strong wind
tore the mountains and broke in pieces the rocks before the Lord,
but the Lord was not in the wind. And after the wind an earthquake,
but the Lord was not in the earthquake. And after the earthquake a fire,
but the Lord was not in the fire. And after the fire the sound of
a low whisper."- 1king 19:11-12 ESV.

The scripture passage above has always fascinated me. Elijah, a prophet in the old testament, has just hurried off to hide in a cave. The Lord then speaks to him and enquires what is going on (as if He didn't already know). Elijah informs the Lord all the other prophets have been killed, and the Israelites have turned their backs on God. I'm sure Elijah was feeling pretty defeated, broken, and lost at this moment. God then humbly shows himself to Elijah, but I'm guessing not in a way that Elijah had expected; a mighty wind passed by, but the Lord was not in the wind. An earthquake shook the mountain, and a fire raged, but God was not in either of those displays. Then Elijah heard a whisper; Ah, there God was, Elijah found God.

The God who created the universe showed Himself to Elijah. God was not found in a bold or grand display of power but in a quiet whisper. God has a way of whispering to His people's hearts in the midst of chaos. The world may be falling apart, and life may seem to be going nowhere, but God is still with you; the question is, will you give Him some of your time and let him whisper to your heart?

Lord, I need You. I quiet my soul and my mind and turn my heart toward You; I am ready to sit and listen for Your whisper, Amen.

TAKE SOME TIME TO BE
QUIET BEFORE THE LORD.
WRITE DOWN ANYTHING YOU
FEEL HE HAS SHOWN YOU.

Day 48. Saved

"How kind the Lord is!"
(Lord, thank you for Your kindness)

" How good he is!"
(Even in the midst of chaos, You are still a good God.)

" So merciful, this God of ours!"
(God, thank you for the mercy You have shown to me.)

*" The Lord protects those of childlike faith; I was facing death,
and he saved me."*
(Lord, teach me to have childlike faith, thank you for the life
You have given me through the death and resurrection of Jesus.)

"Let my soul be at rest again, for the Lord has been good to me."
(I quiet my mind and my soul before You,
I will rest in the truth of Your goodness.)

*"He has saved me from death, my eyes from tears,
my feet from stumbling."*
(Jesus, thank you for saving me from death, You are a good God.)

"And so I walk in the Lord's presence as I live here on earth!"
- Psalms 116:5-9 NLT.
(Lord, I choose to seek Your presence, I long to know You more.)

JESUS, I WANT YOU TO KNOW:

Day 49. Surrounded

"I will bless the Lord who guides me: even at night my heart instructs me. I know the LORD is always with me. I will not be shaken, for he is right beside me." - Psalm 16:7-8 NLT.

Surrounded... through the valley of loss, it may feel like you are surrounded. The walls may feel like they are closing in. Perhaps loneliness and despair are trying to overwhelm you, or fear has lingered, causing anxiety to crash in on you. As you walk through this season, it can be overwhelming to sort through all the thoughts and emotions surrounding you. Do me a favor; pause for a second and take a deep breath. Now let's look at the truth; yes, you are surrounded because all of heaven is on your side.

You are surrounded by heaven; the Lord is with you, His Holy Spirit dwells with you, and His angels have been commanded to go before you and behind you. Yes, you are surrounded. The enemy would love to have you focus on the chaos but remind yourself that the Prince of Peace covers you. When confusion tries to grab hold of your mind, stand firm on the knowledge that the Lord is with you. If depression tries to take control of your emotions, hold on to the truth; you are not alone. The Lord is with you. When you feel it takes too much strength to hold everything together, let it all go, and give it to the Lord.

Take some time each day to fix your focus on Jesus; turn on your favorite worship song and spend a few minutes reminding yourself that you are surrounded by heaven.

Dear Jesus, I take my eyes off the heaviness around me and choose to fix my eyes on You. Help me to remember that I am surrounded by heaven, amen.

HEY GOD,
I AM FEELING...

Day 50. You Will Guide Me

"I will bless the Lord who guides me;
even at night my heart instructs me."

(Lord, Thank you for guiding me. Even while I sleep,
You are instructing my heart.)

"I know the Lord is always with me."

(You are always with me, I am never alone.)

"I will not be shaken, for he is right beside me."

(I throw away the lie that I am alone, I will stand firm on that truth.)

"No wonder my heart is glad, and I rejoice."

(Lord, I choose to walk in joy;
I worship You because You are a good God.)

"My body rests in safety."

(I rest in Your safety; You are with me, and I will not be afraid.)

"For you will not leave my soul among the dead or allow your holy one
to rot in the grave." Psalm 16:7-10 NLT.

(I will not fear; thank you for being with me even in the valley
of the shadow of death. Nothing will separate me from Your love.)

IF YOU COULD TEXT GOD RIGHT NOW, WHAT WOULD YOU TEXT HIM?

HOW WOULD YOU REPLY?

_____

_____

_____

_____

_____

_____

_____

_____

_____

_____

_____

_____

_____

Day 51. Rest

"I wait quietly before God, for my victory comes from him. He alone is my rock and my salvation, my fortress where I will never be shaken."
Psalm 62:1-2 NLT.

Our bodies were designed to need rest; there is nothing better than, after a long, busy day, crawling into one's bed and having a good night's sleep. What about those afternoon naps, the kind where you wake up feeling as if you slept for hours and now could accomplish anything? Just like your body craves rest, so does your soul.

Your soul longs for rest, rest from the craziness of the world. Unlike your body, your soul will not feel at rest from taking a nap or binge-watching your favorite series. Your soul longs and craves for a moment with the Creator. God designed you to dwell in a relationship with Him, and He longs to meet with you. If you feel as though your soul has walked through the desert, take a moment to drink
from the stream of Living Water- the presence of Jesus.

When you feel your soul becoming weary, find a quiet place, just be still and allow your soul to rest in the presence of the Lord. In that time of rest, do not worry about the things that need to be fixed or the problems that seem too large to carry; simply rest. Give your worries to the Lord, then lay down your burdens and remind yourself of the goodness of God. He will be your Rock and your safe place. He longs to meet with you.

Dear Jesus, I set aside my worries, concerns, and troubles
and give them to You. Teach me to allow my soul to rest.
Thank you for being the restorer of my soul.
You are my rock and my fortress, amen.

LORD,
I WANT YOU TO KNOW...

Day. 52 Quiet

"Let all that I am wait quietly before God, for my hope is in him."

(Lord, teach me to wait quietly before You; You are my hope.)

*"He alone is my rock and my salvation, my fortress where
I will not be shaken."*

(You are my rock and my salvation, my safe place.
You will keep me safe.)

"My victory and honor come from God alone."

(Thank you for Your victory, You are a good and righteous Father.)

"He is my refuge, a rock where no enemy can reach me."

(You are my safe place, thank you for keeping me safe.)

"O my people, trust in him at all times."

(Lord, I trust You, I trust that You are a God who keeps His promises.)

"Pour out your heart to him, for God is our refuge."
Psalm 62: 5-8 NLT.

(Lord, thank you that my heart is safe with you.)

LORD, MY HEART FEELS...

Day. 53 Remember

"I will remember the deeds of the Lord; yes, I will remember your wonders of old. I will ponder all your work, and meditate on your mighty deeds."
- Psalm 77:11-12 ESV.

Do you remember the Isrealites struggle to get out of Egypt and to the promised land? God delivered them from the wrath for Pharaoh, parted the Red Sea, and provided for them as they wandered in the desert for 40 years. These people saw God perform miracle after miracle and despite their disobedience, He continued to rescue them. When it came time for the Isrealites to head toward the promised land after spending 40 years in the desert, they once again had to cross a raging river. Again the Lord performed another gravity defying wonder and parted the waters for Isrealites to cross. After the nation of Israel crossed over the Jordan river, the Lord told Joshua to to set up stones as a memorial so that the future generations would know what the Lord had done for them while crossing the Jordan river (Joshua 4:1-8).

Time and time again the Lord commanded the Isrealites to do something in remembrance of what He had done for them. Why would the Lord do that? It was because He didn't want them to forget His faithfulness. He knew many trials and tribulations would come and He wanted His people to be able to say, "remember that time God saved our people for the Egyptians? He can surely save us now!" Or "Remember when our people were hungry and the Lord provided food from heaven. He is a God who provides, and He will provide for us now!"

As you move through this season of grief, set up "stones of remembrance" for yourself. Write down the things you have seen God do in your life, or in the life of those around you. When you feel discouraged or like you may not even know if God is real, take a minute and remember the things the Lord has done.

Jesus, help me to remember your faithfulness, You are good God, amen.

WHAT DO YOU NEED TO REMEMBER?

Day 54. Stronger With You

"For I can do everything through Christ, who gives me strength."
- Philippians 4:13 NLT.

(Lord, you are my strength. No matter what happens, I know I can overcome any obstacle because You are with me.)

"A final word: Be strong in the Lord and in his mighty power."

(Lord, Thank you that because of You, I am strong.)

"Put on all of God's armor so that you will be able to stand firm against all strategies of the devil."

(Thank you for giving me everything I need to stand firm against the devil's strategies.)

"For we are not fighting against flesh-and-blood enemies, but against evil rulers and authorities of the unseen world, against mighty powers in this dark world, and against evil spirits in the heavenly places."
Ephesians 6:10-12 NLT.

(I recognize that there is a battle going on in the spiritual realm.
I take up my weapons of prayer, worship, and the Your Word.
Lord, teach me how to fight well.
Thank you that all of heaven is on my side.)

IN WHAT AREA OF YOUR LIFE DO YOU NEED THE LORD'S HELP?

Day 55. Light in the Darkness

"The Word gave life to everything that was created, and his life brought light to everyone. The light shines in the darkness, and the darkness can never extinguish it." - John 1:4-5 NLT.

Have you ever been in a completely dark room? It's disorienting; finding the light switch in a familiar space can be challenging. Once a source of light has been found, everything instantly seems to make sense; you know where you are and can identify and move around the objects that were once a hazard in the dark. Sometimes grief can feel like being in a dark room, disorienting, confusing, and scary. What can be done about this?

Turn toward The Light; John 1:4-5 describes Jesus as the light of the world. Jesus came to shine a light into the darkness. The interesting thing about light is that it can take over the dark, but the darkness can never take over the light in a room. Jesus is the light in the darkness. In the chaos and confusion, seek his face.

As you walk through this season of loss, allow the Lord to shine his light in the darkest places of your heart. Letting the light of Jesus into a situation doesn't make the problems go away, just like when you turn on the light in a room, the room doesn't change, but your perception of the room changes. As you fix your eyes on Jesus, the loss is still the same, the grief is still valid, but hopelessness will change to hope, despair will change to peace, and sorrow will turn to joy.

Dear Jesus, you are the light of the world, and I need you to shine your light in my heart. I choose to focus on you. I want everything you have for me and my life. Lord, heal the pain and the sorrow; I give you my brokenness and ask for your light to radiate in my heart, Amen.

JESUS,
I WANT YOU TO KNOW….

_____

_____

_____

_____

_____

_____

_____

_____

_____

_____

_____

_____

_____

_____

Day 56. The Light of The World

"In the beginning the Word already existed."

Jesus, you are the Living Word and have been
since the beginning of time.)

"The Word was with God, and the Word was God."

(You were with God as the world was formed, and you are God.)

"He existed in the beginning with God."

(You are the Creator! You spoke the world into existence and
planned my existence!)

*"God created everything through him, and nothing was created except
through him."*

(I am in awe of your creativity, nothing would exist without you.)

*"The Word gave life to everything that was created, and his life brought
light to everyone."*

(Because of you, I have breath in my lungs, thank you for my life. You
are the light of the world!)

*"The light shines in the darkness,   and the darkness can never extinguish
it." - John 1:1-5 NLT.*

(Jesus, you are the light that shines in the darkness; not even death
could stop you.)

GOD, I NEED YOUR HELP BECAUSE….

_____

_____

_____

_____

_____

_____

_____

_____

_____

_____

_____

_____

_____

_____

Day 57. Waves of Grief

"The ropes of death entangled me; floods of destruction swept over me.
The grave[a] wrapped its ropes around me; death laid a trap in my path.
But in my distress I cried out to the Lord; yes, I prayed to my God for
help.
He heard me from his sanctuary; my cry to him reached his ears."
- Psalms 18:16 NLT.

Like the waves crash against the shoreline, so can grief crash within a moment. What do I mean by that? As life seems to return to the new "normal," everything will seem fine, then crash; a memory comes flooding back or that little sting of loss comes rushing back. Sometimes those waves will hit at the most inopportune times, causing a swarm of swirling thoughts and feelings.

When those waves come, don't fight the current of emotions; allow yourself to feel and miss the past. Fighting the waves of grief will not resolve the pain. Just as the waves crash upon the shore, pulling the contents of the ocean's floor up onto the beach, so do the waves of grief clean the soul. A loss is a loss, no matter how small it may be. The key to grieving well is not how little to cry, but being able to grieve with grace, grace for yourself and those around you.

As the waves of grief come and go, the Lord will send his grace. As sorrow flows and questions are wondered, the peace and grace of the Lord will also rush in like the rising tide; seeping in and covering the sand that once was tumbled. The grace of the Lord will be sufficient, and his peace will be abundantly present.

Jesus, help me to navigate the waves of grief; I need your peace
and grace to flood my heart as I wade through this season in life.
Thank you that you have promised never to leave me
or forsake me, amen.

JESUS,
I NEED YOUR PEACE FOR….

Day 58. Even In the Flood Waters

"The ropes of death entangled me; floods of destruction swept over me."
(Lord, some days are really hard, it feels like I am being swept away, but I know you are with me. You will never fail me.)

"The grave[a] wrapped its ropes around me; death laid a trap in my path."
(It feels like this loss is all-consuming and that nothing good will come, but I know it is not true because you are a good God.)

"But in my distress I cried out to the Lord; yes, I prayed to my God for help."
(Thank you for hearing my cries and being my helper in times of distress.)

"He heard me from his sanctuary; my cry to him reached his ears."
- Psalms 18:16 NLT.

"God's way is perfect."
(God, your ways are perfect, although I may not always understand.)

"All the Lord's promises prove true."
(Thank you for always keeping your promises.)

"He is a shield for all who look to him for protection."
(Thank you for protecting me, you are my safe place.)

"For who is God except the Lord?"
(There is no one like you.)

"Who but our God is a solid rock?" - Psalms 18:30-31 NLT.
(You are my firm foundation, and I will not be shaken.)

GOD, TODAY I FEEL...

Day 59. Trust Issues

"Trust in the Lord with all your heart; do not depend on your own understanding. Seek his will in all you do, and he will show you which path to take." - Proverbs 3:5 NLT.

Trust is defined as: "Assured reliance on the character, ability, strength, or truth of someone or something." (Merriam-Webster. (n.d)). As you have weathered the valley of loss, sometimes one's ability to trust can be damaged. It's easy enough to say, "Oh yeah, I trust you," but when it comes down to really putting your trust in something or someone, is your heart actually willing to trust that person? Loss can trigger a need to protect oneself from pain. Perhaps you have told yourself, "Don't let _____ in; they may just leave." Or maybe you have even found yourself having a hard time trusting God.

How can you trust Him when your heart has been so hurt? The people in your life will not be perfect; when one has "trust issues," it can be easy to have high expectations and quickly to toss people aside if they come up short. If you're finding it hard to trust people, here are a few questions to ask yourself; 1) do they have good character? 2) Are they reliable? 3) Are they a truthful person? 4) Do they have my best interests at heart? If you can answer yes to all four of these, then they are likely a person who is worth trusting. Don't allow a bad experience to ruin your future relationships.

If you're struggling to trust the Lord in this season, dig deep into the Bible; I promise you will be able to determine that He is trustworthy. God is for you and will never abandon you. He is a perfect God whose children live in an imperfect world, but if you lean into Him and trust His will, He will lead you.

Jesus, I choose to trust You and Your plans for me. I want everything You have for me. Help me to trust those You have placed in my life, and help me protect my heart from those who will hurt it, amen.

LORD, I TRUST YOU WITH...

Day 60. Trust Goes Both Ways.

"Never let loyalty and kindness leave you!"
(Lord, teach me never to let loyalty and kindness leave me.
Help me to be a trustworthy person.)

"Tie them around your neck as a reminder."
(Help me to remember to always be loyal and kind
to those around me. I want to be a safe place for others)

"Write them deep within your heart."
(I will allow your attributes of kindness and loyalty
to soak deep into my heart.)

*"Then you will find favor with both God and people,
and you will earn a good reputation."*
(I pray that I will find favor both in your eyes and the eyes of those
around me.)

*"Trust in the Lord with all your heart;
do not depend on your own understanding."*
(Lord, I chose to trust you with all my heart.
I will not depend on myself to get it all figured out.)

"Seek his will in all you do, and he will show you which path to take." -
Proverbs 3:5-6 NLT.
(Lord, I chose to seek your will above my own.
Show me the right path to take.)

ARE YOU A PERSON WHO OTHERS CAN TRUST?

_____

_____

_____

_____

_____

_____

_____

_____

_____

_____

_____

_____

_____

_____

IS THERE ANYONE IN YOUR LIFE WHOM YOU NEED TO ASK FOR FORGIVENESS FOR NOT BEING A TRUSTWORTHY FRIEND/FAMILY MEMBER?

_____

_____

_____

_____

_____

_____

_____

_____

_____

_____

_____

_____

_____

_____

PART 3:
ACCEPTANCE
AND
MOVING FORWARD

Day 61. Never the Same

"Jesus Christ is the same yesterday, today, and forever."
- Hebrews 13:8 NLT.

Life will never be the same again; this is a reality you will face many times throughout your life. Life will never be the same after you graduate, it will never be the same after you get married or once you have kids, and it will never be the same after you have experienced a loss. Throughout life, change will always come, and it can be scary.

The loss of someone or a relationship is an unwelcomed kind of change, and often a forced or unexpected change. It can be easy to get stuck in a mindset of constantly fixating on what you have lost, and don't get me wrong, it is okay to mourn that life will never be the same; for a time. But there will come a moment where you have to accept the changes. You don't have to forget the loss, but you have to find peace again. This loss has changed your life, and you may not have the power to change the situation, but you will have the ability to decide how you allow it to change you. Will you become bitter?
Or will you be an overcomer?

Through the constant changes that occur in life, one thing will always remain the same: Jesus; "Jesus Christ is the same yesterday, today, and forever. (Hebrews 13:8 NLT). God's promises will never change, and He will never leave you or forsake you. He will be with you
in this season of change, and He will be your strength
to overcome every change that comes your way.

Dear Jesus, this change is challenging, but I want to overcome the loss and rise out of this valley as an overcomer. You are a good Father, and I trust in your promise that you will be my strength. I ask right now that you will fill me with your peace, Amen.

I AM AN OVERCOMER
BECAUSE….

_____

_____

_____

_____

_____

_____

_____

_____

_____

_____

_____

_____

_____

_____

_____

Day 62. Fixed On You

"For the Lord your God is living among you."

(Lord, You are with me! You are active and living!)

"He is a mighty savior."

(You are a mighty savior; You are my Savior.)

"He will take delight in you with gladness."

(Thank you for caring about the condition of my heart.)

"With his love, he will calm all your fears.[b]"

(Thank you for calming my fears with Your love.)

"He will rejoice over you with joyful songs." - Zephaniah 3:17 NLT.

(Thank you for rejoicing over me with joyful songs,
I ask that you fill my heart with Your joy.)

LORD, I AM WORRIED ABOUT….

_____

_____

_____

_____

_____

_____

_____

_____

_____

_____

_____

_____

_____

_____

LORD, I GIVE YOU MY WORRY AND ASK FOR YOUR PEACE TO FILL ME.

_____

_____

_____

_____

_____

_____

_____

_____

_____

_____

_____

_____

_____

_____

_____

_____

Day 63. Where Do I Go From Here?

*"Trust in the Lord with all your heart; do not depend on
your own understanding. Seek his will in all you do, and he will
show you which path to take." - Proverbs 3: 5-6 NLT.*

The valley of loss has led you on a journey with many twists and
turns; it's probably been messy and filled with raw emotions,
but now what? You don't want to stay in the valley forever;
it's time to hike out of the valley; It's time to move forward.

It's time to move past the rawness of loss and move toward what is
next. I want to make something clear; moving forward doesn't mean
forgetting; you will never forget, and should never forget the person
or relationship you lost. Moving forward means that this loss will
not hold you back from experiencing all that Jesus has for you.
He is a good Father and has great things planned for you.

But how does one move forward? You move forward one day at a
time and with a heart ready to intentionally seek the Lord. When
you open your eyes first thing in the morning, before your feet even
hit the floor, take a moment to reflect on the goodness of God.
Take a moment to be still and ask the Lord what he wants
to show you that day. As you seek him, you will find him.

There is a beautiful life for you, ready to be embraced. There will be
days when you feel fantastic, but there probably will be days
when a wave of grief will hit you again, like a surfer caught off guard
by an eight-foot wave. That's okay, ride the wave,
and then get back up again.

*Jesus, help me move forward. I want everything you have for me.
Thank you for being with me in the valley of grief and being with me
as I hike toward the next part of my journey, amen.*

WHAT DO YOU THINK WILL BE NEXT IN YOUR JOURNEY?

Day 64. Seek and Find

"Seek the Kingdom of God above all else, and live righteously, and he will give you everything you need."

(Lord, teach me how to live righteously and to seek your kingdom. Thank you for providing my every need.)

"So don't worry about tomorrow, for tomorrow will bring its own worries. Today's trouble is enough for today."
-Matthew 6:33-34 NLT.

(Lord, help me not to worry about tomorrow.
I give you my worry and anxiety about the future.)
I choose to focus on one day at a time.)

"Search for the Lord and for his strength; continually seek him."

(Lord, I will search for You and Your strength.)

"Remember the wonders he has performed, his miracles, and the rulings he has given, you children of his servant Israel, you descendants of Jacob, his chosen ones."
- 1 Chronicles 16:11-12 NLT.

(I will remember the wonders You have performed!
I will remember and cling to the laws you gave to
Your chosen people.)

LORD,
I WANT YOU TO KNOW….

_____

_____

_____

_____

_____

_____

_____

_____

_____

_____

_____

_____

_____

_____

_____

_____

Day 65. A New Season

"For everything there is a season, a time for every activity under heaven."
- Ecclesiastes 3:1 NLT.

As King Solomon so poetically wrote, there is a season for everything; a season to cry, a season to laugh, a season to dance, and a season to grieve (Ecclesiastes 3). Just as the winter changes to spring and the spring changes to summer and then to fall, you too will go through many different seasons in life. Some seasons will be incredible, and other seasons in life will be difficult, but remember that there is a place for all the seasons and a space for all the feelings in those seasons.

As you have just weathered a season of grief, the time will come for a new season. You can not stay stuck in a season of grief forever, and changes that have occurred in life must be accepted; you must move forward. Joy must come again, just like the rain must come in the spring after a quiet winter.

As you leave this season of grief, know that just because one moves forward in life does not mean you have to forget about the loss, but that you are simply moving forward in healing your heart. Hold on to Jesus, hold on to your beloved memories, and let go of the daily sorrow. I pray that as you move forward that your tears will turn to laughter, and your grief be turned to dancing. I pray that the joy of the Lord will fill you, and that new life and new dreams will grow within your heart.

Dear Jesus, I pray that you will fill me with your peace as I walk out of this season of grief. Lord, show me how to navigate through this change of season well. I pray that your joy will be my strength, amen.

IF YOU COULD SEND GOD A TEXT, WHAT WOULD YOU SAY?

_____

_____

_____

_____

_____

_____

_____

_____

_____

_____

_____

_____

_____

_____

HOW WOULD HE RESPOND?

Day 66. Trusting In Your Plans

"'For I know the plans I have for you," says the Lord."

(As I walk into this new season of life, I choose to trust
in the plans You have for me.)

*"They are plans for good and not for disaster, to give you
a future and a hope."*

(I know your plans for me are good; I trust You.
I know that if disaster comes, you will be with me.
Thank you that in you, I have a future and hope.)

" In those days when you pray, I will listen."

(Thank you for hearing my prayers.)

" If you look for me wholeheartedly, you will find me."
Jeremiah 29:11-13 NLT.

(Lord, I seek you with my whole heart,
I want to know you,
and I want everything you have for me.)

WHAT DO YOU NEED TO TRUST THE LORD WITH IN THIS NEW SEASON OF LIFE?

Day 67. Guilt Free

"So now there is no condemnation for those who belong to Christ Jesus. And because you belong to him, the power of the life-giving Spirit has freed you from the power of sin that leads to death."
- Romans 8:1-2 NLT.

As you begin to trudge your way out of the valley of loss, the devil would like nothing more than to pull you back down into that dark valley. Why am I even talking about the devil? Because the devil doesn't want you to live life abundantly, and he may try very hard to trick you into being stuck in his pit of despair. He may be a master manipulator but isn't very creative and often uses the same old tricks. If I can make you aware of his schemes, perhaps you can avoid his traps altogether.

The devil often tries to drown his targets in guilt and condemnation. The devil loves to make you feel guilty; as you move forward, watch out for this thought; "oh, how can you be okay when _____ happened? You shouldn't be enjoying yourself." Does this sound like a familiar thought? Another way he likes to sneak his way in is by finding a way to bring condemnation into your life, "It's your fault _____ happened," or " you should have done _____, and everything would have been okay." Tricky little thoughts like this can cause a lot of damage to one's heart.

If you ever feel weighed down by guilt or condemnation, do yourself a favor and throw those heavy thoughts away. Combat the lies with the truth; there is no condemnation for those who are in Christ Jesus (Romans 8:1), and the Lord created you to live life abundantly (John 10:10)! Do not let the devil trick you back into grief.

Jesus, thank you that I do not have to live with guilt or condemnation. I rebuke the spirit of guilt and condemnation, they have no place in my life, and I replace those feelings with your love and peace, amen.

JESUS, I GIVE YOU....

Day 68. Freedom

"So now there is no condemnation for those who belong to Christ Jesus."

(Thank you that I do not have to live under condemnation. I break off all guilt and condemnation; they are not my inheritance.)

"And because you belong to him, the power of the life-giving Spirit has freed you from the power of sin that leads to death." - Romans 8:1-2 NLT.

(Thank you, Jesus, that I belong to you and have freedom through your Spirit. The power of sin has no hold on me!)

"For this is how God loved the world: He gave his one and only Son, so that everyone who believes in him will not perish but have eternal life."

(Lord, thank you for loving me and sending your Son to die for me. Thank you for the gift of eternal life.)

" God sent his Son into the world not to judge the world, but to save the world through him." - John 3:16-17 NLT.

(God, you are a good Father, thank you for the gift of salvation.)

Day 69. Thankfulness: A Weapon Against Despair

*"Always be joyful. Never stop praying. Be thankful in all circumstances,
for this is God's will for you who belong to Christ Jesus."*
1 Thessalonians 5:16-18 NLT.

"In everything, give thanks?" Yes, in everything, give thanks. "Even in this situation?" Yes, especially in the midst of loss. Why does the Bible instruct us to give thanks in every situation? It doesn't seem to make sense, and to modern society, it may not make sense, but thankfulness is a powerful weapon. A heart of Thankfulness has the ability to drive out despair.

Regardless of your circumstances, you have a choice, and that choice is that you get to choose how you position your heart. Will you position yourself to allow your circumstances to pull you into despair? Or will you position your heart in a posture that looks up toward the Lord? Thankfulness can shift your focus from your struggles and fixate it on the positive aspects of life, and on to the giver of life; Jesus. Now, I'm not saying that you have to be thankful for the loss you have experienced, but search for something to be thankful for.

If you feel yourself falling into a pit of despair, take a few moments to genuinely thank God for something. Your Thankfulness doesn't need to be anything grand, you can simply be thankful for the breath in your lungs, or the warm bed you sleep in. A   Thankful heart is a key to contentment, and contentment is a key to living a joy-filled life in Jesus.

Dear Jesus, thank you for the air in my lungs and thank you for this day that I have been blessed with. Teach me to walk in a spirit of thankfulness; I want to live a joy-filled life, Amen.

LORD, I AM THANKFUL FOR...

Day 70. Give Thanks

"Praise the Lord!"

(Lord, you are a good Father and worthy to be praised!)

"Give thanks to the Lord, for he is good!"

(Thank you for your goodness, you are a good God.)

"His faithful love endures forever."

(You are so faithful to love me no matter what I do.
Thank you for your faithful love that endures forever!)

"Who can list the glorious miracles of the Lord?"

(You are a God who works miracles, open my eyes
to recognize your miraculous deeds.)

" Who can ever praise him enough?"

(I can't even begin to praise you enough, you are a good God.)

*"There is joy for those who deal justly with others and always do
what is right." - Psalm 106:1-3 NLT.*

(Lord, fill me with your joy, teach me to live my life justly,
and help me be convinced to do what is right in Your eyes.)

Day 71. Alpha and Omega

"' I am the Alpha and the Omega—the beginning and the end," says the Lord God. "I am the one who is, who always was, and who is still to come—the Almighty One.'" - Revelation 1:8 NLT.

In the scriptures, God is referred to as the Alpha and the Omega, the beginning and the end. He was God in the beginning; when He formed the foundations of this world, He will still be God in the end. The God who created the universe also created you. He knew you before He formed the world, chose you (Ephesians 1:4), and wants to be a part of your story.

In fact, He is still writing your story, and this is not the end. He has great things planned for your life. If you allow Him to, He will take the brokenness you have experienced and use it for good. I have seen Him do it time and time again as I have allowed the Lord to lead and guide me. I can confidently say that I have seen the Lord take my brokenness and turn it into something beautiful. Will you partner with Him and allow the Lord to work through you and your story?

When you partner with Jesus, something beautiful will come out of your story. As you walk through life, share your story; even if your life only impacts one person, that person can impact someone else, and so on, a ripple effect can be created. Jesus is not done with your story; if there is still breath in your lungs, there is so much more. Keep trusting in the Lord with your story.

Dear Lord, I recognize that you are the Alpha and Omega- the beginning and the end. I know You have chosen me for such a time as this, and I choose to trust You with my story. I want everything You have for me, and I want my life to reflect Your life, amen.

JESUS, I WANT YOU TO KNOW...

Day 72. Run the Race Well.

"Therefore, since we are surrounded by such a huge crowd of witnesses to the life of faith, let us strip off every weight that slows us down, especially the sin that so easily trips us up."

(Lord, strip away anything slowing me down, especially any sin that has tripped me up.)

"And let us run with endurance the race God has set before us."

(I want to run my race with endurance. I want my story to be a testimony of Your faithfulness.)

"We do this by keeping our eyes on Jesus, the champion who initiates and perfects our faith."

(I fix my eyes on You, Jesus, the one who guides me and perfects my faith.)

"Because of the joy awaiting him, he endured the cross, disregarding its shame."

(Thank you for enduring the cross and dying for my sins.)

"Now he is seated in the place of honor beside God's throne."
- Hebrews 12:1-2 NLT.

(I sit here in awe of what You have done for me, Jesus. You overcame the sins of the world and now sit in a place of honor beside the throne of God. You are a good God.)

IS ANYTHING HOLDING YOU BACK FROM RUNNING THE RACE THE LORD SET BEFORE YOU?

Day 73. God of the Past, Present, and Future

"Teach these new disciples to obey all the commands I have given you. And be sure of this: I am with you always, even to the end of the age." - Matthew 28:20 NLT.

Before Jesus left this earth, he gave his disciples special instruction, known as the great commission. He commanded them to go into all the nations and to make disciples (Matthew 28:18-20). At the end of his great commission speech, he said, "And be sure of this; I am with you always, even to the end of the age." (Matthew 28:20). This promise remains true; not just for his twelve disciples, but for all who follow him. The Lord is with you.

As you have walked through the valley of loss, Jesus was with you. He is still with you, and his promise will remain true for your future. The Lord has never left you or forsaken you, and he will never leave or forsake you. After a season of change, it may be hard to walk forward in your journey, but keep pressing on and keep your eyes on the Lord. He is with you.

Do not let your heart be troubled with what tomorrow may bring; the Lord will guide your steps, give him all the worries of the future. Remember how He has provided for you in the past, and simply focus on the present. He is the God of your past, present, and future.

Dear Jesus, thank you for promising never to leave or forsake me. Thank you for being with me in the past and that you are still with me now. I am so thankful that You will be with me in the future, amen.

LORD, I AM WORRIED ABOUT...

LORD, I GIVE YOU MY WORRIES.

_____

_____

_____

_____

_____

_____

_____

_____

_____

_____

_____

_____

_____

_____

_____

Day 74. My God is Worthy

"I will exalt you, my God and King, and praise your name forever and ever."

(You are my God and my King, I will praise your name forever!)

"I will praise you every day; yes, I will praise you forever."

(Lord, You are worthy, I will praise You every day, You are so worthy.)

"Great is the Lord! He is most worthy of praise!"

(You are a great God; there is no one like You! You are worthy of all my praise.)

"No one can measure his greatness."

(There is no way for me to begin to understand how great You are!)

"Let each generation tell its children of your mighty acts; let them proclaim your power."

(Jesus, I pray that every generation in my family will know You and Your power.)

"I will meditate on your majestic, glorious splendor and your wonderful miracles." - Psalm 145:1-5 NLT.

(I will fix my focus on You and Your glorious splendor, I will not forget that You are a miracle-working God!)

LORD,
I WANT YOU TO KNOW...

_____

_____

_____

_____

_____

_____

_____

_____

_____

_____

_____

_____

_____

_____

_____

Day 75. For His Glory

"Then your salvation will come like the dawn, and your wounds will quickly heal. Your godliness will lead you forward, and the glory of the Lord will protect you from behind."- Isaiah 58:8 NLT.

If you have spent any time around the church, I am sure you have heard this verse: "And we know that in all things God works for the good of those who love him, who have been called according to his purpose." (Romans 8:28 NIV). But how can this be when trauma, heartache, and suffering are all an inevitable part of the human experience? How can loss and grief work out for good?

As I have walked through life and experienced loss and heartache, I have come to this conclusion; no matter what happens, my God will be glorified. "And they overcame him [Satan] by the blood of the Lamb and by the word of their testimony, and they did not love their lives to the death." (Revelation 12:11 - NKJV). Every obstacle I overcome means I have one more testimony to help others find healing and freedom. Nothing is more beautiful than seeing someone find freedom in Jesus; this is when good comes out of sorrow.

Because of Jesus's redemption, you can rise above the darkness. Because of Jesus's love, He will heal your wounds, and as you cling to Him, your faith will shine as a testimony to a lost and hurting world. If you let the Lord, He will turn this sorrow into a story of redemption. Are you willing to allow the Lord to use this sorrow for His glory?

Jesus, I trust that You can take my loss and grief and redeem it for Your glory. I ask that every part of my life will shine for Your glory. I pray that in this, the world will see that You are God, amen.

WRITE YOUR TESTIMONY:

_____

_____

_____

_____

_____

_____

_____

_____

_____

_____

_____

_____

_____

_____

Day 76. By The Word of Their Testimony

"Then your salvation will come like the dawn, and your wounds will quickly heal."

(Jesus, thank you for my salvation, thank you that you are healing my heart.)

" Your godliness will lead you forward, and the glory of the Lord will protect you from behind."- Isaiah 58:8 NLT.

(I trust You because You are a good God. Thank you for leading me through this valley. Thank you for protecting me.)

"And they overcame him [Satan] by the blood of the Lamb and by the word of their testimony, and they did not love their lives to the death." - Revelation 12:11 NKJV.

(Because of Your redemption, I am an overcomer.
I pray that my testimony will shine Your glory
and help others find freedom in You, Jesus.)

"And we know that in all things God works for the good of those who love him, who have been called according to his purpose." - Romans 8:28 NIV.

(Thank you that I am called, I trust that You will take my brokenness and use it for good.)

JESUS, TODAY I FEEL...

Day 77. My Confidence

" Yet I am confident I will see the Lord's goodness while I am here in the land of the living."- Psalm 27:13 NLT.

Picture this; Joseph, sitting at the bottom of a pit, looks up to see that his brothers who threw him in had finally returned. When he is pulled out, he discovers he is not being recused but is being sold off as a slave. That, my friend, is a very lousy day. Once in Egypt, Joseph is sold again as a servant, where he works his way up and becomes the head servant of the household. However, his master's wife l ies about his character, which lands Joseph in prison; Joseph had it rough.

It would be easy to feel pretty discouraged if one was in Joseph's situation, but despite his circumstances, Joseph still chose to believe in the Lord's promises for his life. What if Joseph had given up? What if he had said, "forget this. I'm done with you, God." It would be a fair assumption to speculate that all of Egypt and the descendants of Jacob (a vital part of the lineage of Jesus) would have been wiped out by famine. Thankfully, Joseph didn't give up; he knew God was faithful. Joseph had confidence in his God, and because of his simple obedience, he was eventually released from prison and put in charge of the entire country of Egypt! Joseph was reunited with his family and saved them and all of Egypt from the famine. Yes, Joseph saw the goodness of God fulfilled (Genesis 37-46).

Right now, you may feel like you are in a pit or a prison, like Joseph, and it could be easy to sink into discouragement. Instead of sinking, stand in confidence, knowing that even though you may not see it now, you will see the goodness of God here on earth. He is always faithful.

Dear Jesus, I stand confidently, knowing I will see your goodness and faithfulness here on earth just like Joseph. I trust you, amen.

WHAT ARE SOME GOOD THINGS GOD HAS DONE IN YOUR LIFE?

Day 78. Holding My Head Up High

"For he will conceal me there when troubles come;
he will hide me in his sanctuary."
(Lord, thank you for being my safe place, I will hide and rest
in your presence.)

"He will place me out of reach on a high rock."
(Thank you for keeping me safe.)

"Then I will hold my head high above my enemies who surround me."
(I will hold my head high because you are with me.)

"At his sanctuary I will offer sacrifices with shouts of joy,
singing and praising the Lord with music."
(I rest in your presence and worship you because you are
worthy of being praised.)

"Hear me as I pray, O Lord."
(Thank you for hearing my prayers.)

"Be merciful and answer me!"
(Thank you for being merciful and that you will answer me.)

"My heart has heard you say, "Come and talk with me.""
(Thank you for being a God who longs to have a relationship with
me.)

" And my heart responds, "Lord, I am coming."" - Psalm 27: 5-8 NLT.
(Lord, I choose to spend time in your presence.)

HOW HAVE YOU SEEN THE LORD'S PRESENCE IN YOUR LIFE?

Day 79. Stay Close

"Your word is a lamp to guide my feet and a light for my path."
- Psalm 119:105 NLT.

Have you ever heard a parent tell their child to "stay close," Perhaps at an amusement park or a store? This is a common phrase of instruction that parents give their children to alert them of the possibility of danger or chaos. If the child heeds the instructions and the parent keeps a close eye on their child, the trip will probably be peaceful and uneventful. But if the child chooses to stray away, they may find themselves lost.

Like a parent reminds a child to stay close, the Lord also reminds His children to stay close. As the path of life is filled with unexpected twists and turns, it is important to pay extra attention to seek the Lord during these times. People often get lost and lose their faith in the twists and turns. Hebrews 11:6 NLT says, "And it is impossible to please God without faith. Anyone who wants to come to him must believe that God exists and that he rewards those who sincerely seek him."

As you continue to work through the journey of processing your grief, actively pursue the Lord. Unplug from all distractions; that bing-worthy show can wait for another 10 minutes. Turn off that phone and feed your soul. When the stress feels like it is piling high, turn on the worship tunes and crack open that bible. When the path seems unclear, the word of the Lord will light your path.

Jesus, I give you my full attention; I choose to stay close to You.
I want everything You have for me, and I trust You.
I know that if I seek You, I will find You, amen.

HOW DO YOU FEEL YOUR RELATIONSHIP WITH THE LORD IS?

Day 80. Your Word

"I have refused to walk on any evil path, so that I may remain obedient to your word."

(Lord, I refuse to love the sin in this world, help me to remain obedient to Your word.)

"I haven't turned away from your regulations, for you have taught me well."

(I know that in your laws, there is life and peace, teach me to continue to learn how to walk in Your ways.)

"How sweet your words taste to me; they are sweeter than honey."

(Your words are pure and true, they are sweeter than honey.)

" Your commandments give me understanding; no wonder I hate every false way of life."

(Despite what the world tries to tell me, what is right and wrong, I know that your commandments are true, I chose to stand firm in the truth of your word.)

"Your word is a lamp to guide my feet and a light for my path."
- Psalm 119: 101-105 NLT.

(Your word is like a light in the darkness, showing me how to live a life that honors You; thank you for giving me Your word.)

HEY GOD,
I WANT YOU TO KNOW...

Day 81. Mourning Into Joy

"You have turned my mourning into joyful dancing.
You have taken away my clothes of mourning and clothed me with joy,
that I might sing praises to you and not be silent. O Lord my God,
I will give you thanks forever!"
- Psalm 30: 11-12 NLT.

When grief hits, it can feel like the whole world has gone dark; joy may feel like it will never be found again. Joy is an interesting concept; it is often confused with the emotion of happiness, but it's not a feeling based on circumstances. Joy comes from a deep well within one's soul. It is a fruit of the Holy Spirit.

As a fruit of the Holy Spirit, it is something that one must learn to cultivate in their soul. The joy of the Lord is not snuffed out when things go wrong but remains as a source of strength (Nehemiah 8:10). Yes, you will mourn, and that is okay; there is a season for that, but continue to cultivate a joy-filled heart.

How can one cultivate a joy-filled heart in the midst of grief? Firstly, allow yourself time to grieve, then fix your eyes on the promise of Jesus. Regardless of what happens on earth, the joy of the Lord can be found. When discouragement comes, practice finding joy. When sorrow comes, find a reason to thank the Lord, and perhaps when no one is looking, turn on your favorite song and dance away; you may just find a little bit of joy return.

Jesus, thank you that my mourning will turn to joy. I give you my sorrow and ask for your joy to fill my soul. Teach me to live a joy-filled life as I navigate this season of loss, amen.

GOD, I WANT YOU TO KNOW...

Day 82. Fill Me Up With Joy!

"To all who mourn in Israel, he will give a crown of beauty for ashes, a joyous blessing instead of mourning, festive praise instead of despair."

(Lord, thank you that You will give me a crown of beauty instead of ashes. I ask You to provide me with a joyous blessing instead of mourning and that You will replace any despair with a heart of praise.)

"In their righteousness, they will be like great oaks   that the Lord has planted for his own glory." - Isaiah 61:3 NLT.

(Lord, teach me to stand in righteousness like a great and mighty oak)

" You have turned my mourning into joyful dancing."

(Lord, I trust in You and thank You that my mourning will turn to joyful dancing.)

" You have taken away my clothes of mourning and clothed me with joy, that I might sing praises to you and not be silent."

(Lord, I ask that you will fill me with your joy and that I will praise you and not be silent.)

" O Lord my God, I will give you thanks forever!"
- Psalm 30: 11-12 NLT.

(You are my God, I will praise You and give thanks to You forever.)

IF YOU COULD TEXT GOD RIGHT NOW, WHAT WOULD YOU TEXT HIM?

_____

_____

_____

_____

_____

_____

_____

_____

_____

_____

_____

_____

_____

_____

_____

_____

Day 83. A New Thing

"For I am about to do something new. See, I have already begun! Do you not see it? I will make a pathway through the wilderness. I will create rivers in the dry wasteland." - Isaiah 43:16 NLT.

Transition is a tough place to be in; you're stuck between the old and the new, just waiting for things to happen. Perhaps anxiously anticipating the new season or dreading the changes about to take place, and maybe a little bit of both. That moment of transitioning from one stage of life to the next is often when the realization hits; life will never be the same.

Grief is like a dry wasteland, one in which you never asked to travel, and changes have occurred that you probably never thought would happen. However, despite the loss, life keeps going; time keeps ticking. As you continue to move forward from the past and toward the future, know that the Lord is with you. He is making a path out of this wilderness for you, and something new will come. As you move toward the new life that lies before you, it's okay to grieve the change and embrace them as well.

As the new things come, continue to walk in grace, not only for those around you but for yourself as well. If anxiousness begins to rise,
take a moment to breathe and seek out the peace of the Lord. You do not have to navigate this new journey alone, the Lord is with you, and he will guide you if you allow him to.

Dear Jesus, I give you my worries and any anxiousness that I may have about the future. I choose to rejoice in the new things coming, even though it may sting a little. I trust that you are with me. Help to walk in grace and in Your peace, amen.

WHAT ARE YOU SCARED ABOUT AS YOU MOVE TOWARD A NEW CHAPTER IN LIFE?

_____

_____

_____

_____

_____

_____

_____

_____

_____

_____

_____

_____

_____

_____

_____

WHAT ARE YOU
EXCITED ABOUT?

Day 84. New

"For I am about to do something new."
(Lord, thank you that You are constantly working on my behalf.
Thank you for the new things you'll bring into my life.)

" See, I have already begun! Do you not see it?"
(Lord, open my eyes to see Your plans for me and the new things
You have begun to do in my life.)

" I will make a pathway through the wilderness."
(Thank you for being a God who makes pathways
through the wilderness.)

"I will create rivers in the dry wasteland."
- Isaiah 43:16 NLT
(Thank you for providing for me in this season of grief;
You are a good Father.)

"He has given me a new song to sing, a hymn of praise to our God."
(Lord, You are worthy to be praised, I will worship You.)

"Many will see what he has done and be amazed."
(I pray that many will see what You have done and realize
that You are a good God.)

" They will put their trust in the Lord."
- Psalm 40:3 NLT
(Lord, I put my trust in You.)

GOD, I FEEL...

Day 85. Wisdom

"If you need wisdom, ask our generous God, and he will give it to you. He will not rebuke you for asking." - James 1:4-5 NLT

Left? Right? Back? Forward? Should I say this? Should I do that? What do I do? Where do I go from here? All these questions may fly through your mind as you navigate the changes that have occurred in your life. It can be overwhelming and confusing to try and "figure things out." You may not need to figure it all out, But there will be times in life when you will have to make some tough decisions, so start praying for wisdom now.

Wisdom is a gift from God that He promises to give to those who ask for it (James 1:4). When Solomon became king, he was just a child, and the Lord asked him what he would want to be given. Solomon replied that he wanted wisdom to govern his people well and justly. This request pleased the Lord, and not only did He promise to provide him with wisdom, but He also promised to make him a wealthy and famous king. A king that would never be forgotten (1 Kings 3:9-14).
If you seek the Lord and ask for wisdom, He will give it to you. It will then be up to you to decide to follow that wisdom. I can reassure you that no one has ever regretted praying for wisdom.

Jesus, thank you for being a God who keeps His promises.
Jesus, I ask that You will fill me up with wisdom.
I want everything You have for me,
I love You, and I trust You, amen.

GOD, I NEED WISDOM FOR...

Day 86. Just Ask

"If you need wisdom, ask our generous God, and he will give it to you.
He will not rebuke you for asking." - James 1:4-5 NLT
(Lord, I need Your wisdom; thank you for the promise
of wisdom to all who ask.)

"Keep on asking, and you will receive what you ask for."
(Lord, teach me to pray fervently. Thank you for being my provider.
You will provide me with everything I need.)

"Keep on seeking, and you will find."
(I will press into You in prayer, and I know that will find You.)

"Keep on knocking, and the door will be opened to you."
(Lord, I will seek You and Your wisdom
until my prayers are answered.)

"For everyone who asks, receives."
(Thank you for hearing my prayers
and for the wisdom I will receive.)

" Everyone who seeks, finds."
(Thank you that everyone who seeks you will find you.)

"And to everyone who knocks, the door will be opened."
- Matthew 7:7-8 NLT.
(Thank you for hearing my prayers and answering them.)

WHAT ARE YOU PRAYING FOR RIGHT NOW?

JESUS WILL ANSWER YOUR PRAYERS; SOMETIMES, HIS ANSWERS ARE "YES," "NO," OR "WAIT." HOW DO YOU FEEL THE LORD HAS RESPONDED TO YOUR PRAYER?

_____

_____

_____

_____

_____

_____

_____

_____

_____

_____

_____

_____

_____

_____

_____

Day 87. Worry Less

"Give all your worries and cares to God, for he cares about you."
- 1 Peter 5:7 NLT.

You may have heard the phrase, "pray more, worry less!"
It's a cheesy saying, I know, but that doesn't mean it's not true.
Worrying less is much easier said than done; trust me, I would know,
I am a "certified overthinker." It's hard not to worry about what will
happen in the future, and it's also hard not to worry about what
could happen to our friends and family. There are so many scenarios
that could or could not happen. How does one overcome worry?

First, one needs to recognize the source of the worry; is it fear
of loss, Fear of the unknown, or fear of things being out of your
control? Many sources could be the root of your worry, but the
keyword here is fear. In order to stop worrying, you must figure out
where the fear is coming from. Fear can be all-consuming, causing
anxiety to fill one's entire being. Fear is not your friend; it is a tactic
from the enemy
to distract you from God's bigger plans.

In Matthew 6:25-34, Jesus discusses the topic of worry.
To summarize His words of wisdom, I will quote Him on this,
"Can any one of you by worrying add a single hour to your life?"
(Matthew 6:27 NIV) Worrying adds nothing to your life other than
more worry and anxiety, "give your worries and care to the Lord, for
he cares for you," (1 Peter 5:7 NLT). Now is the time to train your
mind to let go of the things you can't control and focus on the things
you can control. When worry and fear creep in, kick them out,
and replace that space with fiery prayers.

Jesus, I give you my worries and fear. I kick them out! Teach me to pray
instead of worry, amen.

WHAT IS SOMETHING YOU ARE CURRENTLY WORRIED ABOUT THAT YOU NEED TO GIVE TO THE LORD?

Day 88. Kick Out The Worry!

"Don't worry about anything; instead, pray about everything."
(Lord, help me remember to pray about everything
when I am worried.)

" Tell God what you need, and thank him for all he has done."
(Lord I need _____, thank you for _____.)

*"Then you will experience God's peace, which exceeds anything
we can understand."*
(Lord, I recognize that your peace comes through prayer
and a thankful heart.)

" His peace will guard your hearts and minds as you live in Christ Jesus."
(I pray that your peace will guard my heart and mind through
Christ Jesus)

*" And now, dear brothers and sisters, one final thing. Fix your thoughts
on what is true, and honorable, and right, and pure,
and lovely, and admirable."*
(I choose to focus on what is true, honorable, right, pure,
lovely, and admirable.)

" Think about things that are excellent and worthy of praise."
- Philippians 4:6-8 NLT.
(I choose to fix my mind on things that are excellent
and worthy of praise.)

Day 89. Next

"Therefore, go and make disciples of all the nations,[b] baptizing them in the name of the Father and the Son and the Holy Spirit."
Matthew 28:19 NLT.

Before Jesus ascended to heaven, He met with His disciples one last time. Jesus had one more important message for them; He gave them what is now known as the Great Commission. Jesus said, "'I have been given all authority in heaven and on earth. Therefore, go and make disciples of all the nations,[b] baptizing them in the name of the Father and the Son and the Holy Spirit. Teach these new disciples to obey all the commands I have given you. And be sure of this:
I am with you always, even to the end of the age.'" (Matthew 28:18-20). This beautiful commission was not just for His disciples but for you as well!

As a follower of Jesus, the great commission is just as much for you as it was for the disciples. The Lord has given you authority in heaven and on earth. He has called you to teach others about Him, the Father, And the Holy Spirit. As you have navigated this season of grief, I pray that you have grown in your relationship with the Lord, and I hope you have been filled with faith. The Lord has great plans for you and longs to partner with you to bring His love to others.

The last thing Jesus said before he went up to heaven was, "'and be sure of this: I am with you always, even to the end of the age.'" (Matthew 28:20 NLT.) As you move forward, out of the valley of loss, I pray you will never forget the Lord's promise to always be with you! He was with you in the valley and will be with you on the mountain tops. Never forget, you are never alone.

Jesus, give me the courage to step out in this new season.
I want to use my story to help other people see that You are God, amen.

GOD I WANT YOU TO KNOW...

Day 90. Commissioned

"I have been given all authority in heaven and on earth."

(Lord, I recognize that Your word says that you have given me authority in heaven and on earth. Teach me to walk in that authority.)

"Therefore, go and make disciples of all the nations,[b] baptizing them in the name of the Father and the Son and the Holy Spirit."

(Lord, I want to be used by You, help me to show the people around me who You are.)

"Teach these new disciples to obey all the commands I have given you."

(As I walk in obedience to your commands, help me to be an example and teach those around me how to obey and honor your commands.)

"And be sure of this: I am with you always, even to the end of the age."
- Matthew 28:18-20 NLT.

(Thank you for always promising to be with me, even to the end of the age.)

WRITE DOWN SOMETHING YOU HAVE LEARNED THROUGH THIS DEVOTIONAL. WHAT IS SOMETHING YOU NEVER WANT TO FORGET?

_____

_____

_____

_____

_____

_____

_____

_____

_____

_____

_____

_____

_____

_____

As we conclude this grief and loss devotional, we stand at the intersection of human suffering and divine hope. Our journey through the stages of grief has taken us through deep valleys and steep mountains, as we have navigated the profound pain of loss. Yet, amidst our tears and heartache, we have discovered that even in the darkest of times, the light of God's Word shines through, offering solace, comfort, and a pathway to healing.

May the peace of God, which surpasses all understanding, guard your hearts and minds in Christ Jesus (Philippians 4:7).

Amen.

TAKE A MOMENT TO REFLECT
ON THE PAST 90 DAYS.
HOW WERE YOU FEELING
BEFORE EMBARKING ON
THIS JOURNEY, AND HOW
DO YOU FEEL NOW? WHAT
VALUABLE LESSONS HAVE
YOU LEARNED, AND HAS
YOUR FRIENDSHIP WITH GOD
GROWN STRONGER?

_____

_____

_____

_____

_____

_____

_____

_____

_____

_____

Made in United States
North Haven, CT
27 June 2023

38295601R00122